A Christmas Gift
of Grace

An Amish Holiday Romance

Sylvia Price

Penn and Ink Writing, LLC

Contents

Stay Up to Date with Sylvia Price

Subscribe to Sylvia's newsletter at newsletter.sylviaprice.com to get to know Sylvia and her family. It's also a great way to stay in the loop about new releases, freebies, promos, and more.

As a thank-you, you will receive several FREE exclusive short stories that aren't available for purchase.

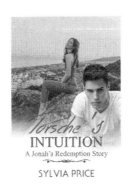

Praise for Sylvia Price's Books

"Author Sylvia Price wrote a storyline that enthralled me. The characters are unique in their own way, which made it more interesting. I highly recommend reading this book. I'll be reading more of Author Sylvia Price's books."

"You can see the love of the main characters and the love that the author has for the main characters and her writing. This book is so wonderful. I cannot wait to read more from this beautiful writer."

"The storyline caught my attention from the very beginning and kept me interested throughout the entire book. I loved the chemistry between the characters."

"A wonderful, sweet and clean story with strong characters. Now I just need to know what happens next!"

"First time reading this author, and I'm very impressed! I love feeling the godliness of this story."

"This was a wonderful story that reminded me of a glorious God we have."

"I encourage all to read this uplifting story of faith and friendship."

"I love Sylvia's books because they are filled with love and faith."

Other Books by Sylvia Price

**Sarah (The Amish of Morrissey
County Prequel)** – FREE
**Sadie (The Amish of Morrissey County
Book 1)** – http://getbook.at/sadie
**Bridget (The Amish of Morrissey County
Book 2)** – http://getbook.at/bridget
**Abigail (The Amish of Morrissey County Book
3)** – http://getbook.at/morrisseyabigail
**Eliza (The Amish of Morrissey County
Book 4)** – http://getbook.at/eliza
**Dorothy (An Amish of Morrissey County
Christmas Romance)** – http://getbook.at/dorothy
The Amish of Morrissey County Boxed Set
– http://mybook.to/morrisseybox

**The Origins of Cardinal Hill (The Amish
of Cardinal Hill Prequel)** – FREE
**The Beekeeper's Calendar (The Amish
of Cardinal Hill Book 1)** –
http://getbook.at/beekeeperscalendar

The Soapmaker's Recipe (The Amish of Cardinal Hill Book 2) – http://getbook.at/soapmakersrecipe
The Herbalist's Remedy (The Amish of Cardinal Hill Book 3) – http://getbook.at/herbalistsremedy
The Amish of Cardinal Hill Complete Series – http://mybook.at/cardinalbox

∞ ∞ ∞

A Promised Tomorrow (The Yoder Family Saga Prequel) – FREE
Peace for Yesterday (The Yoder Family Saga Book 1) – http://getbook.at/peaceforyesterday
A Path for Tomorrow (The Yoder Family Saga Book 2) – http://getbook.at/pathfortomorrow
Faith for the Future (The Yoder Family Saga Book 3) – http://getbook.at/faithforthefuture
Patience for the Present (The Yoder Family Saga Book 4) – http://getbook.at/patienceforthepresent
Return to Yesterday (The Yoder Family Saga Book 5) – http://getbook.at/returntoyesterday
The Yoder Family Saga Boxed – http://getbook.at/yoderbox

∞ ∞ ∞

An Amish Christmas in Whispering Pines –
http://mybook.to/whisperingpines

∞ ∞ ∞

*The Christmas Cards: An Amish Holiday
Romance* – http://getbook.at/christmascards

∞ ∞ ∞

*The Christmas Arrival: An Amish Holiday
Romance* – http://getbook.at/christmasarrival

∞ ∞ ∞

*Seeds of Spring Love (Amish Love
Through the Seasons Book 1)* – http://
getbook.at/seedsofspring
*Sprouts of Summer Love (Amish Love
Through the Seasons Book 2)* – http://
getbook.at/sproutsofsummer
*Fruits of Fall Love (Amish Love Through the
Seasons Book 3)* – http://getbook.at/fruitsoffall
*Waiting for Winter Love (Amish Love
Through the Seasons Book 4)* – http://
getbook.at/waitingforwinter
Amish Love Through the Seasons Boxed Set
– http://getbook.at/amishseasons

∞ ∞ ∞

Jonah's Redemption: Book 1 – FREE
Jonah's Redemption: Book 2 –
http://getbook.at/jonah2
Jonah's Redemption: Book 3 –
http://getbook.at/jonah3
Jonah's Redemption: Book 4 –
http://getbook.at/jonah4
Jonah's Redemption: Book 5 –
http://getbook.at/jonah5
Jonah's Redemption Boxed Set –
http://getbook.at/jonahset

∞ ∞ ∞

*Elijah: An Amish Story of Crime and
Romance* – http://getbook.at/elijah

∞ ∞ ∞

*Finding Healing (Rainbow Haven
Beach Prequel)* – FREE
*Finding Hope (Rainbow Haven Beach Book
1)* – http://mybook.to/rhfindinghope
*Finding Peace (Rainbow Haven Beach Book
2)* – http://mybook.to/rhfindingpeace

Finding Love (Rainbow Haven Beach Book 3) – http://mybook.to/rhfindinglove
Finding Home (Rainbow Haven Beach Book 4) – http://mybook.to/rhfindinghome
Finding Joy (Rainbow Haven Beach Book 5) – http://mybook.to/rhfindingjoy
Finding Faith (Rainbow Haven Beach Book 6) – http://mybook.to/rhfindingfaith
Christmas at Rainbow Haven (Rainbow Haven Beach Book 7) – http://mybook.to/rhchristmas

∞ ∞ ∞

Songbird Cottage Beginnings (Pleasant Bay Prequel) – FREE
The Songbird Cottage (Pleasant Bay Book 1) – http://getbook.at/songbirdcottage
Return to Songbird Cottage (Pleasant Bay Book 2) – http://getbook.at/returntosongbird
Escape to Songbird Cottage (Pleasant Bay Book 3) – http://getbook.at/escapetosongbird
Secrets of Songbird Cottage (Pleasant Bay Book 4) – http://getbook.at/secretsofsongbird
Seasons at Songbird Cottage (Pleasant Bay Book 5) – http://getbook.at/seasonsatsongbird
The Songbird Cottage Boxed Set – http://getbook.at/songbirdbox

∞ ∞ ∞

The Crystal Crescent Inn (Sambro Lighthouse Book 1) – http://getbook.at/cci1
The Crystal Crescent Inn (Sambro Lighthouse Book 2) – http://getbook.at/cci2
The Crystal Crescent Inn (Sambro Lighthouse Book 3) – http://getbook.at/cci3
The Crystal Crescent Inn (Sambro Lighthouse Book 4) – http://getbook.at/cci4
The Crystal Crescent Inn (Sambro Lighthouse Book 5) – http://getbook.at/cci5
The Crystal Crescent Inn Boxed Set – http://getbook.at/ccibox

Unofficial Glossary of Pennsylvania Dutch Words

Ach – Oh

Appeditlich – delicious

Bis widder – Until (we meet) again (a parting phrase)

Boppli – baby

Bruder – brother

Daed – dad

Danki – thanks

Dochder – daughter

Eldre – parents

Familye – family

Fraa – wife/woman

Frehlicher Grischtdaag – Merry Christmas

Gaern gschehne – You're welcome

Gmay – local Amish -community

Gott – God

Grischtnacht – Christmas Eve

Gude daag – Hello (literally Good day)

Gude mariye – Good morning

Gude nacht – Good night

Gude naamidaag – Good afternoon

Guder owed – Good evening

Gut – good

Kapp – Amish head covering

Kind/Kinner – child/children

Kumm – come

Liewi – dear

Maedel – girl

Maem – mom

Mann – husband/man

Menner – men

Nee – no

Neffyu – nephew

Niess – niece

Onkel – uncle

Schweschder – sister

Sei gut – Be good (a parting phrase)

Soh – son

Vadder – father

Weiwer – women

Willkumm – welcome

Wunderbaar – wonderful

Ya – yes

Prologue

C lutching the tiny quilt she had sewn for her daughter, Grace, against her petite frame, Mary Fisher stood in her daughter's bedroom. Once a haven of anticipation and joy, the room now felt like a mausoleum of lost dreams. The plain wooden bed frame, hand-carved by Isaac, stood in one corner, its emptiness a poignant reminder of the future they had envisioned. Framed embroidery pieces bearing Bible verses, each carefully crafted by the women in the community, bedecked the soft cream walls. The handmade rocking chair, where Mary had once sat and softly sung lullabies to her daughter, now stood idle.

The silence in the room was almost tangible. Mary traced the embroidered flowers on the quilt, fingers trembling; each stitch was a labor of love, each thread a testament to the hope she had once held for her daughter. Tears welled up in her hazel eyes, but she blinked them back, her grief held at bay by a floodwall, which if opened, she feared would be too vast and in which she'd be left adrift.

Her thoughts were interrupted by the sound of a saw—Isaac in his workshop; the place that had become his sanctuary since Grace's passing. The loss of their daughter had created an uncrossable chasm between Mary and Isaac. Once, their bond had been a source of strength, their shared faith, a pillar of support. Now, Isaac's emotional distance only deepened her isolation. He had thrown himself into his work, repairing the barn and tending to furniture, trying to outrun his pain. Their conversations had dwindled to monosyllables and polite nods, the warmth and affection they once shared seemingly evaporated.

Mary's memories drifted back to the first

signs of Grace's illness: a persistent cough and a slight fever. They had dismissed it as a common cold, nothing to worry about. But as days turned into weeks, Grace's condition worsened. Her once rosy cheeks grew pale, and her bright eyes became dull and listless. Doctors' visits became more frequent, each one bringing more worry than relief.

When the local doctor had done all he could, they were granted permission by the bishop to travel to the hospital for further tests. Mary vividly recalled the day they received the diagnosis. She and Isaac had sat in the doctor's office, the cloying smell of antiseptic clinging to the air. The doctor's words were clinical and devoid of emotion: a rare and aggressive childhood cancer, a battle Grace's small body might not win. The room had seemed to close in on them, the heaviness of the news crushing their spirits.

They had returned home in silence, the gravity of the situation sinking in. There was no treatment available that they could afford and none that was likely to work even if they could. That night, Mary and Isaac had knelt beside Grace's bed with their hands clasped tightly in prayer. They pleaded with God to spare their little girl, to grant them a miracle. Mary's heart had ached with a desperation never experienced by her before or since. Each whispered prayer was a lifeline thrown out in hope and faith.

But as the days passed, Grace's condition only deteriorated. Her once vibrant energy dwindled until it became naught, her laughter a distant memory. Mary had watched, helpless, as Grace withered before her eyes—a summer tree in full bloom being stripped of its vivid color and giving way to the naked skeletal branches of winter. Each day, Grace grew weaker, her small body frail and fragile.

Mary spent countless hours at Grace's bedside, singing lullabies and telling stories, trying to bring comfort to her in any way she could. She would hold Grace's small hand, feeling the life slipping away, and fight back tears, determined to be strong for her little girl. Isaac, too, had been a constant presence, his face etched with grief and helplessness.

Then one evening, as Mary sat by the window with Grace in her arms, she felt a profound stillness in the air. Grace looked up at her with those big beautiful eyes, a fleeting spark of recognition and love. Mary had whispered words of comfort, telling Grace it was okay to let go, that she would always be loved, always be remembered. And with a final soft sigh, Grace closed her eyes, the struggle leaving her body as she found peace. She'd gone to God, leaving Mary alone.

"Mary," Isaac said softly.

She turned to face him, clutching the edge of the bed. Mary's bleary gaze focused on Isaac as he stood in the doorway, his tall lean frame casting a shadow. He was shaped by years of hard work, his strong, calloused hands bearing testament to countless hours of woodworking. Each line and scar on his hands told a story, a history of dedication and skill that Mary had always admired.

Isaac's short dark brown hair was neatly trimmed, though it was often hidden beneath the wide-brimmed hat he wore when working outside. His deep blue eyes, which had once sparkled with joy and mischief, now reflected a mix of sadness and determination. They were eyes that had seen much, eyes that carried the weight of their shared sorrow.

Mary had always found comfort in Isaac's presence, in the steady strength he exuded. But now, as she looked at him, a pang of guilt and frustration churned in her belly. She discerned the worry etched into his features, the pain he tried so hard to hide. Isaac was a good man, a devoted husband, and a loving father. Yet, in their grief, man and wife seemed to be drifting further and further apart.

"I didn't make supper," she admitted, her voice barely more than a whisper.

Isaac nodded, his face expressionless. The thick silence hung between them. Mary knew she was failing as a wife and as a partner, but the thought of returning to normalcy felt like a betrayal. If she moved on, wouldn't Grace's memory begin to slip away until it faded completely?

"I'm worried about you," Isaac said finally. "You should go and sit by the fire, not seclude yourself in this cold room."

Mary shook her head, her long chestnut braid swaying against her back.

Isaac hesitated, his brow furrowing in concern. He took a step closer, his voice gentle but firm. "Perhaps we should donate Grace's things to the local orphanage," he hedged. "The *kinner* could use them, especially with *Grischtdaag* coming."

Mary's heart clenched violently. "You want to give away her things?" she asked incredulously, her voice rising in her distress. "As if she never existed?"

Isaac sighed, running a hand through his hair. "*Nee*, Mary. I'm not trying to pretend that our *dochder* never existed. But we can't go on like this. Grace is gone; she's with *Gott*. We need to find a way to live again."

Tears welled up in Mary's eyes as she shook her head vehemently. "You don't understand, Isaac. You just don't understand a *maem's* grief."

Isaac's face tightened. "I do understand grief, Mary. I lost her, too. But look at this place. It's falling apart, and so are you. You hardly eat. You don't get dressed. This isn't living."

Mary's hands trembled as she gripped the bed's edge. "She was our miracle, Isaac. We tried for years to have *kinner*, and then Grace came along. She was my greatest dream. And now she's gone."

Isaac stepped forward, reaching to take her hand, but she pulled away. "Mary," he said, his voice breaking. "I miss her, too. Every single day. But we have to find a way to keep going, for her memory, for us."

Mary turned away, tears streaming down her face. "I can't, Isaac. I just can't."

Ever since Grace passed, they'd been drifting, but right at that moment, the distance between them felt insurmountable, a chasm widened by their different stages of grieving. Isaac stood there for a moment, his shoulders slumped in defeat. "I'm here when you're ready to talk," he said softly before turning and leaving the room.

As the door closed behind him, Mary sank to the floor, hugging the quilt to her chest. The weight of her sorrow was overwhelming, suffocating. She knew Isaac was right, that they couldn't continue like that. But the thought of moving on, of letting go of Grace's things, felt impossible.

In the cold, quiet bedroom, Mary wept, her tears soaking into the quilt she had sewn with so much love. She prayed for strength, for a way to heal, and for the grace to bridge the gap between her and Isaac. But all she could feel was the profound emptiness left by Grace's absence and the agonizing reality that moving forward might mean letting go.

Chapter One

One Month Later

The aroma of freshly baked bread filled the small cozy bakery, mingling with the sweet scent of pastries and cookies. Wooden shelves lined the walls, bursting with a tantalizing array of homemade goods: loaves of rye and whole wheat bread, jars of preserves and honey, and rows of pies with golden, flaky crusts. The counter, polished to a warm sheen, offered a selection of cookies, muffins, and sweet rolls, all artfully arranged.

Hannah Weaver moved swiftly around the room, her hands deftly handling the hot trays. She pulled a tray of golden-brown cinnamon rolls from the oven, their tops glistening with a light drizzle of icing. The heat brushed against her face, making her cheeks flush as she set the tray on the cooling rack.

Across the room, Mrs. Miriam Bontrager, an elderly woman with a kind face, was serving a customer. Her gray hair peeked out from beneath her *kapp*, and her eyes crinkled warmly as she wrapped up a loaf of bread. The bell above the door jingled a soft greeting as another customer entered.

Hannah nimbly packed a basket with a loaf of sourdough bread, a few cinnamon rolls, some oatmeal cookies, and a small jar of apple butter. Once the basket was ready, she walked over to Mrs. Bontrager.

"I'm going to take this over to the Fishers," she said, her voice soft but resolute. "I shouldn't be long."

Mrs. Bontrager looked up from her task, her eyes shining with understanding. "Take your time, *liewi*," she said gently.

Hannah nodded gratefully. "*Danki*, Mrs. Bontrager. I'll be back as soon as I can."

Basket in hand, Hannah stepped out of the bakery. She paused, adjusting her shawl against the cold, and took in the bustling scene of Willowvale.

The town, nestled in a picturesque valley,

was a quaint portrait of the simple life they led. Modest wooden houses with neatly trimmed gardens lined the streets. Smoke curled from chimneys, filling the air with the nostalgic scent of wood fires. The snow that had fallen the night before blanketed the ground, sparkling under the soft winter sun.

Hannah started down Main Street, walking leisurely down the snow-covered path. The town was alive with activity. Children, bundled in heavy coats and woolen scarves, ran about, their laughter echoing through the crisp air. Some were building snowmen, while others engaged in playful snowball fights. Their joy was infectious, and Hannah couldn't help but smile.

The general store was busy, as it always was that time of year. Families were stocking up on supplies, preparing for the holiday season. Through the window, Hannah spied Mr. Yoder, the storekeeper, chatting with a customer while his wife wrapped parcels with practiced efficiency. Wreaths of evergreen decorated doorways, and red ribbons added a festive touch.

The rhythmic clanging of metal rang out as she passed the blacksmith's shop, a steady, reassuring sound. The iron artisan, a burly man named Elmo, paused from his work to send a nod and warm smile Hannah's way.

"*Gude mariye*, Hannah!" he called over the din.

"*Gude mariye*, Elmo," she replied, her warm breath evident against the backdrop of chilly air.

As Hannah continued toward the Fishers' house, the basket swayed gently on her arm. The bright morning sun cast a golden light over Willowvale that contrasted sharply with the sorrow that had settled over the Fisher household since the previous fall. Little Grace's loss affected the entire community. Everyone missed the cheerful six-year-old girl who once brought so much joy into their lives.

Hannah had interceded in prayer for the Fishers every day, hoping they would find solace firstly in their faith and then in each other. But word around town was that Mary wasn't doing so well. No one had seen her since the funeral, and Hannah's concern intensified with each passing day. She knew the pain of loss all too well and couldn't bear the thought of Mary suffering alone. That morning, she'd decided to do more than pray. She would visit.

The path to the Fishers' house was familiar,

lined with snow-sprinkled hedges and barren trees. As Hannah approached, she was welcomed by the steady rhythmic sound of hammering coming from Isaac's carpentry workshop.

She walked up the two steps and onto the porch before gently knocking on the door, her heart beating faster with anticipation and apprehension. Moments later, the door creaked open, revealing Mary, whose eyes were red and swollen, her face pale and gaunt. She appeared thin, her night clothes hanging loosely like a circus tent on her petite frame. Ignoring Mary's disheveled appearance, Hannah offered a warm smile and held out the basket.

"*Gude daag,* Mrs. Fisher," she said softly. "I brought you some things from the bakery."

Mary's fingers brushed against Hannah's as she accepted the basket, the touch delicate and tentative. "*Danki*, Hannah," she murmured.

For a moment, neither woman spoke.

"Would you like to *kumm* inside?" Mary finally asked.

Hannah nodded, and Mary stepped aside to let her in. As Hannah stepped over the threshold, the weight of the sorrow within the house enveloped her. The entryway led into a small living room. The furniture, simple and handcrafted, had an air of neglect about it, a thin layer of dust hinting at how little the room was being used. A woven rug, now slightly askew, covered the wooden floor.

The neglect was even more apparent in the kitchen; the kitchen table, usually the heart of Amish homes, was cluttered with unopened mail and unwashed dishes. The stove was cold and idle. The cabinets were neatly closed, but the whole room felt as though it were in a state of suspended animation, waiting for life to return.

Hannah's gaze wandered to the small window above the sink, where delicate lace curtains framed the view of the snow-covered yard. Outside, the wooden swing set that Isaac had built now stood stark and lifeless against the white backdrop. The sight tugged at her heartstrings, a profound reminder of the absence of joy that had once filled the space.

"Would you like some tea?" Mary offered.

"That would be nice," Hannah accepted, smiling.

Hannah sat at the kitchen table, setting the basket on top, and watched as Mary moved to the cupboard. But it was as if she were walking through mud, every step slow and laborious, every action a battle.

She reached for the teapot and cups, her hands trembling slightly. As Mary fumbled with the teapot, Hannah stood up.

"Let me help you with that," she offered, stepping forward.

Mary met her gaze, her eyes welling up with tears. *"Danki,"* she said. "I just...I don't have the energy."

Hannah gently extricated the teapot from Mary's hands and began to prepare the tea. She filled the kettle with water and set it on the stove, then fetched the tea leaves and cups. As she moved about the kitchen, Mary sank into a chair at the table, her body sagging with exhaustion.

Hannah poured the boiling water into the teapot, the steam rising in gentle curls. She placed the teapot and cups on the table and sat down opposite Mary.

"There you go," she said.

"Danki," said Mary, wrapping her hands around the cup.

Seconds ticked by but neither spoke. The metrical thud, thud, thud of Isaac's hammer could be heard in the distance.

"How are things at the bakery?" Mary enquired, her voice laced with wistfulness.

Hannah set her cup down and smiled warmly. "Busy, as always. But I think the cold makes everyone hungrier. We can't seem to bake enough sugar cookies."

Mary's eyes misted over, and she sighed softly. "Grace loved sugar cookies," she said, her voice trembling. "She would always beg for one every time we passed the bakery…"

Her voice trailed off, and Hannah reached across the table, squeezing Mary's hand tenderly. "I remember," she said. "She was such a sweet, spirited *maedel*. We all miss her so much."

Just then, the kitchen door creaked open and Isaac stepped in. He stopped short when he saw Hannah, a look of surprise and pleasure crossing his face. "Hannah," he said, his voice warm but tired. "It's *gut* to see you."

"I brought some things from the bakery," Hannah replied, gesturing to the basket.

Isaac's eyes softened, and he nodded. "*Danki*, Hannah. That's very kind of you."

The kitchen fell silent, the air thick with unspoken words and lingering tension. Hannah could sense the strain between Mary and Isaac.

The silence was heavy and almost palpable, pressing down on them all.

Isaac cleared his throat, his gaze shooting between the two women. "Well, I'll leave you to it," he said, his voice strained. He offered a small tight smile, then excused himself, disappearing through the house.

Hannah watched him go, her heart aching for the couple. She turned back to Mary, who was staring at her tea, the sadness in her expression even more pronounced. Hannah sipped her tea, searching for the right words to offer comfort. She knew how much the community missed seeing Mary and how the church could be a source of solace in times of heartache.

"I hope to see you at church this Sunday," Hannah ventured gently, watching Mary's reaction carefully.

Mary's face fell, and she shook her head slowly. "It's too hard," she whispered, her voice tinged with pain. "I can't bear the looks from the others. The pity in their eyes...it's too much."

Hannah felt a pang of sympathy. She knew the well-meaning concern of the community could sometimes feel overwhelming.

"I understand," she said. "But it might bring

you some comfort. Being surrounded by people who care about you, sharing in the faith that binds us all… it could help."

Mary looked down at her hands, the delicate fingers tracing the rim of her teacup. "*Nee*," she said firmly but quietly. "I can't. Not yet."

The room fell silent again. Hannah's mind raced, desperate to find the right thing to say, something that could ease Mary's pain, even just a little.

She placed her hand over Mary's, feeling the disparate coldness of her skin. "I remember when my *maem* died," Hannah started, her voice gentle and steady. "It's a while ago now, but the memory of that time is still as vivid as though it were but yesterday."

Mary's expression softened, and she nodded, her grip on the teacup tightening. "I remember your *maem*," she said quietly. "She was so kind. Always had a smile for everyone."

Hannah smiled wistfully, her eyes misting over with the memories. "*Ya*, she was. I remember how she used to sing hymns as she worked. And after she was gone, it felt like the light in our home had been snuffed out."

Mary's eyes filled with tears again, but she

seemed to draw some comfort from Hannah's account.

"I know our stories aren't the same," Hannah said, "but over time, I began to see that life could go on, even with the pain. It wasn't easy, but eventually, I found a way to live with the loss."

Mary's tears spilled over, but she didn't look away. "It's so hard, Hannah," she said, her voice cracking. "I don't know how to move forward."

"I know," Hannah replied, her own voice trembling. "And it's okay to feel that way. Grief doesn't have a timeline, and everyone heals in their own time. But you don't have to do it alone."

Mary nodded slowly, the pain in her eyes mingling with a spark of understanding. "*Danki*, Hannah," she said softly.

The kitchen fell silent once more, but Hannah felt the fragile bridge of shared experience begin to solidify between them.

"I'm quite tired," said Mary.

"I will leave you," Hannah said as she stood.

As Hannah turned to go, Mary leaned over and grasped her hand. "Will you *kumm* and visit me again?" she asked.

"Of course," replied Hannah.

Mary managed a small smile as she patted

the back of Hannah's hand softly.

As Hannah left the Fisher house, the cold December air nipped at her cheeks. She glanced back once, her heart heavy with sorrow, before setting off down the snow-shrouded path back toward the bakery. The soft crunch of her boots in the snow was the only sound accompanying her thoughts.

As she walked, Hannah's mind drifted back to those painful years after her mother and brother died. She could still recall the silence that filled their home, one not merely attributable to the absence of her family members but to the unwillingness of her father to engage with the world. Her father, the town bishop, had retreated into himself and his work, leaving her to navigate her grief alone.

Hannah had been a girl on the brink of womanhood when she lost her mother and brother. Their home, once filled with her mother's laughter and the promise of new life, became a place of shadows and unspoken sorrow. She remembered how she would sit in her mother's rocking chair, clutching one of her aprons to her cheek, trying to find a sense of comfort in the fabric that still bore her faint scent.

Her father, though physically present, had been emotionally distant. His duties as bishop consumed him, and his grief built a wall between father and daughter that Hannah didn't know how to scale. He performed his pastoral duties with an almost mechanical precision, his sermons full of wisdom and compassion, but at home, he was a hollow shell of the man he had once been.

For years, Hannah struggled to find her way through life without a mother's guidance and with a father who was there but never truly present. It was only in recent years that her relationship with her father had begun to improve. They were slowly beginning to rebuild their bond, but the scars of those lonely years remained, giving Hannah a deep empathy for Mary's struggle.

She could identify with Mary's loneliness and her inability to find her feet again after losing Grace. Hannah knew the darkness that could envelop a person after such a profound loss and the difficulty of reaching out for help when even the littlest of feats felt like a monumental effort.

As Hannah turned into the main street, the sound of approaching footsteps pulled her from her thoughts. She looked up to see Daniel King, her childhood friend, walking towards her, a broad smile on his face and his sandy blond hair that curled slightly at the edges, escaping from beneath his dark wide-brimmed hat.

"Hannah," Daniel called out, his broad smile holding form. "I was hoping to catch you. I stopped in at the bakery, but Mrs. Bontrager said you had gone out."

"I went to see the Fishers," Hannah explained.

"How are they?" Daniel asked.

Hannah pressed her lips together but said nothing.

"Well, it was kind of you to visit them," he said, his expression softening. "But that is unsurprising; I have never met anyone as kind as you."

"I just took them some things from the bakery," Hannah rationalized.

Daniel smiled and gave a shake of his head. "You've never been *gut* at accepting compliments," he said with a chuckle.

Hannah opened her mouth but closed it

again, unsure of what to say.

"Well, I was wondering when you might take a ride with me in my buggy," Daniel said, his tone light but his eyes hopeful.

Hannah bit her lip. "I'd like that, Daniel, but I've been so busy with work at the bakery," she explained. "And I'm also helping with the school *Grischtdaag* program and my *daed's* annual church charity drive. There just don't seem to be enough hours in the day."

Daniel's cheerful expression fell slightly, disappointment shadowing his features. "I understand," he said, trying to keep his tone upbeat. "You've always been one to take on so much. It's one of the things I admire about you."

Hannah's heart ached at his words, knowing he hoped for more from her than she felt capable of giving.

"Well, just...know that the offer stands whenever you're ready."

Hannah reached out and squeezed his hand, wishing she could ease his disappointment. "You're a *gut* friend, Daniel."

His eyes met hers, and they stood there wordlessly for a moment in the cold. Their friendship had begun when they were just children, chasing each other through the fields and playing hide-and-seek in the barns. Hannah was always the adventurous one, leading Daniel on daring escapades that often ended in fits of laughter. Daniel, for his part, brought a sense of calm and thoughtfulness to their dynamic, balancing Hannah's boundless energy with his steady presence.

As they grew older, their friendship deepened. They worked together on community projects, attended church services side by side, and shared their dreams and fears in the quiet moments between chores. Daniel had been a constant source of support for Hannah during the difficult years after her mother and brother passed away. In recent years, he would often stop by the bakery to lend a hand or simply to check on her, his presence a reassuring reminder that she wasn't alone.

Their bond had always been strong, but as they entered adulthood, the expectations of their community began to loom larger. Riding in a buggy together was more than just a friendly gesture; it signified a potential courtship, a step toward a future together. And while Daniel's feelings for Hannah had clearly deepened,

Hannah found herself at a crossroads, unsure if her feelings for him extended beyond the kind of affection that had defined their relationship for so long.

Daniel's gentle nature and unwavering loyalty had always been a considerable comfort to Hannah, but she couldn't ignore the doubts that nagged at her heart. She valued their friendship deeply and feared that pursuing a romantic relationship might change things irrevocably, especially if her feelings didn't match his.

"I should get back to the bakery," Hannah said.

Daniel nodded.

"I'll see you soon," said Hannah in farewell.

As she walked away, guilt gnawed at her. She cared deeply for Daniel, but she was also fully aware of the significance of riding in the buggy with him. It was more than just a ride; it was a public step toward a deeper commitment, one she wasn't ready for since she wasn't sure if she felt anything beyond platonic friendship for him.

Daniel was a wonderful man, kind and dependable, someone who would make a loving husband. But her heart remained uncertain as to whether she was the woman whose husband he should be.

With a sigh, she pushed the confusing thoughts aside, focusing instead on the tasks ahead. There were cookies to bake, a Christmas program to plan, and a community to support. For the time being, she would pour her energy into those things, hoping that, in time, her heart would find clarity.

Chapter Two

Levi Miller stood at the edge of Willowvale, taking in the serene landscape that stretched out before him. The rolling fields, dusted with a light layer of snow, shimmered under the soft winter sun. As he gazed out over the tranquil beauty of the valley, a flicker of hope that this place might finally bring him the solace he desperately needed sparked in him.

For a moment, his thoughts drifted back to the life he left behind. Just a few months earlier, he had lived in a bustling town, surrounded by the familiar comforts of home and the promise of a bright future. His parents had been his rock, their unwavering support a constant in his life. His fiancée, Emma, had been his heart's desire, her laughter and love filling his days with joy.

But he then discovered firsthand how grief has a way of unraveling even the most carefully woven plans. The sudden loss of his parents had shattered his world, leaving him adrift in a stormy sea of sorrow, feeling as though there was no lifeboat to save him. Emma, though loving and supportive, couldn't understand the depth of his pain, and he'd felt himself slowly but surely being pulled away from her on the riptide of grief, unable to swim against the current and bridge the growing distance between them. The memories of happier times became haunting echoes that he couldn't escape, and soon, his once-perfect life felt like a dream that had been snatched away and left him trapped in a nightmare of the ghosts of memories past.

In his darkest times, his sister's letters were a lifeline. She had moved to Willowvale with her husband years earlier, and her words painted a picture of a place untouched by the harshness of the world, a community bound by faith and simplicity. She wrote of the town's quiet charm and the way it seemed to heal the soul and offer a fresh start. It was her gentle persuasion that had finally prompted Levi to leave everything behind and seek refuge in the serene valley before him.

Now, standing at the threshold of his new beginning, Levi closed his eyes and took a deep breath, filling his lungs with the crisp air. The distant sounds of life reached his ears: the lowing of cattle and a cardinal's call—sounds that were a soothing balm to his weary spirit.

Hitching his satchel up on his back, Levi made his way into the village. As he walked down the snow-coated street, he was struck by the serenity of the place. The stillness was almost palpable, broken only by the occasional clip-clop of a horse's hooves or the distant sounds of children playing. His old town, though still adhering to many Amish principles, had adopted some aspects of modern life. The dissimilarity in Willowvale was profound and glaringly obvious.

The hum of a generator or the glow of electric lights to which he had grown accustomed back home were nonexistent. In his previous town, certain homes and businesses had small discreet generators for essential use, especially during the long winter months when daylight was scarce. The gentle, almost comforting hum of these generators had been a background constant. In Willowvale, however, the only sounds were nature's songs: the rustling of the wind in the bare trees or the accompanying metallic chirp with a flash of red as a Northern Cardinal took flight.

As Levi continued down the main street, he noticed the lack of telephone wires strung between poles. Back in his old town, limited use of telephones had been allowed for business purposes, and the sight of wires crisscrossing the sky was as familiar as the flora. In Willowvale, there were no such intrusions. The skyline was clear and uninterrupted, lending the village an open, expansive feel.

The buildings themselves reflected the commitment to the tradition of the town's people. The homes were simple, painted in muted earthy tones, each with a well-maintained porch and neatly stacked firewood by the door. He passed the general store, its wooden sign swinging gently in the icy breeze, announcing its reason for being with hand-painted letters. By glimpsing inside, he could see shelves lined with jars of preserves, while on the floor stood barrels of flour, oats, and other essentials of daily life.

The blacksmith's shop caught his eye next. It stood sturdy and unyielding, indicative of a craft that had remained unchanged for centuries. The rhythmic clanging of the blacksmith's hammer on the anvil rang out, a satisfying, steady sound that spoke of hard work and skill. Levi paused to watch as the blacksmith expertly shaped a piece of glowing steel, marveling at the man's strength and precision.

Further down the street, he spotted the schoolhouse. The modest building's white walls blended with the snowy landscape. Through the windows, he glimpsed children seated at their desks, their breath puffs visible in the cool air. The teacher, a young woman in a plain dress, moved gracefully among them, guiding their lessons. There were no modern conveniences —no computers or electric lights, just the pure, unadulterated pursuit of the knowledge appropriate to the continuity of their peaceful life.

The quiet, the simplicity, and the steadfast adherence to tradition were both comforting and daunting. He wondered how he would adjust to a life so different from what he had known, but he also felt a stirring of hope. Perhaps in this timeless place, he could finally find the peace and sense of belonging that had eluded him since his parents' passing.

As Levi walked, absorbed in the allure and simplicity of the village, he suddenly collided with someone. The unexpected impact caused the person to drop a basket into the snow as they stumbled to maintain their balance.

"*Ach*, I'm so sorry!" Levi exclaimed, bending down to help retrieve the fallen item.

"*Nee* harm done," a warm gentle voice replied.

Levi looked up to see a beautiful young woman with curly auburn hair peeking out from beneath her *kapp* and striking green eyes that reflected the snowy landscape around them. Her smile lit up her entire face, and despite the almost certain inconvenience he had caused, she radiated a sense of calm and kindness.

Levi's breath caught in his chest as he met her eyes. "I didn't mean to bump into you. I was... a bit distracted," he admitted sheepishly.

She laughed softly, a melodic sound that seemed to warm the frigid air around them. "It's quite all right," she said. "More than once, I have found myself so caught up in my head that I've walked a mile in quite the wrong direction."

Levi smiled.

"I'm Hannah Weaver, by the way. And you are?"

"I'm Levi," he replied, standing up and dusting the snow from his hands. "Levi Miller. I'm on my way to my sister's house, but I think I might have gotten a bit turned around."

Hannah's smile widened. "You must be Rachel's *bruder*. She's mentioned you in our prayer meetings. *Willkumm* to Willowvale."

"*Danki*," said Levi with an appreciative nod.

She adjusted her *kapp* and looked down the street. "Rachel's house is on my way. I'd be happy to take you there."

Levi felt a wave of gratitude mixed with something else he couldn't quite place. "I appreciate it."

As they fell in step together, Hannah started to tell him about the village. Her voice was filled with enthusiasm and affection.

"That house over there"—she pointed to a charming white cottage with a picket fence —"belongs to the Yoder *familye*. They have the best vegetable garden in the village. Mrs. Yoder makes the most amazing pickles and preserves.

You have to try them."

Levi nodded, smiling at her animated expression. "I'll definitely have to do that."

"And that building over there," she continued, pointing to a small building with a sign, "is the Tea Shop. Everyone gathers there to chat and catch up. Mrs. Petersheim runs it. She is without a doubt the sweetest woman you'll ever meet."

He glanced at the tearoom, then back at Hannah.

"And just a bit further down is the bakery where I work," she said. "We make everything from bread to cookies to pies. You should *kumm* by some time. I'll make sure you get a taste of our famous oatmeal molasses biscuits."

Levi found himself unable to tear his eyes away from Hannah. She was captivating, and he felt a kinship and connection that he couldn't quite explain.

Hannah suddenly stopped walking, her cheeks flushing. "I'm talking too much, aren't I? What about you? What brings you to Willowvale?"

Levi hesitated before frankly answering, "A fresh start."

Hannah nodded. "Well, you've *kumm* to the right place."

They fell into silence for a few steps, and Levi cast a sideways glance at Hannah, admiring the gentle arches of her profile. She turned and met his eye, and he quickly looked down, averting his gaze.

"Here we are," Hannah announced, stopping at the gate.

The house was a modest two-story structure made of sturdy timber and painted a soft cream shade that blended in beautifully with the surrounding snowy landscape. The roof was steeply pitched, designed to shed heavy snow, and the wide front porch with its sturdy wooden railing invited visitors to rest and stay awhile.

Wooden shutters framed the windows, and lace curtains peeked out, adding a touch of delicate charm. Neatly stacked firewood was piled by the side of the house. The front yard was well-kept, with a path of flat stones leading up to the porch. Even in the winter, the remnants of a summer garden were visible, with the skeletal structures of trellises and a small snow-covered vegetable patch hinting at the life that would burst forth come spring. A wooden swing hung from the large oak tree in the yard, its snow-dusted seat a quiet promise of warmer days and leisurely afternoons.

Levi turned to Hannah. *"Danki."*

Hannah smiled, her eyes twinkling. "It was my pleasure. I'm sure we'll see each other around."

As she walked away, Levi watched her go, gratitude and curiosity filling his heart. There was something special about her, something that made him feel a little less lost and a lot more hopeful.

When she had disappeared from sight, he turned toward his sister's house. As he approached the front door, his stomach churned. It had been a while since he last saw Rachel—not since their parents' funeral. He took a deep breath and knocked.

Moments later, the door opened, revealing his sister, Rachel Peachey. Her face lit up with a warm smile as she saw him, her brown eyes shimmering with emotion.

"Levi!" she exclaimed, stepping forward without hesitation to embrace him. "It's so *gut* to see you!"

Levi hugged her tightly, feeling the grief of

the past months lift slightly from his shoulders. "It's *gut* to see you, too, Rachel. I've missed you."

Rachel pulled back, her eyes scanning his face with concern. "You found the place all right, then? I was worried."

"I had a little help," Levi confessed.

Rachel smiled. "*Kumm* in, *kumm* in. You must be cold."

She stepped aside to let him enter.

Inside, the house was warm and inviting. The living room was cozy, with handmade quilts draped over the backs of wooden chairs and a large braided rug overlaying the wooden floor. A fire crackled in the hearth, casting a warm light around the room. The walls were decorated with simple, beautiful pieces of Amish craftsmanship, and the smell of freshly baked bread wafted through the air.

Rachel's husband, Conrad, a tall, steadfast man with a kind face and dark hair, rose from his chair. "*Willkumm*, Levi," he said, extending his hand. "It's *gut* to have you here."

Levi shook his hand, detecting the genuine warmth in Conrad's grip. "*Danki*, Conrad."

From behind Conrad, two small faces peeked out. Anna and Eli, Rachel and Conrad's children, were both under ten, with the same light brown hair as their mother and bright curious eyes. Anna, the elder of the two, stepped forward shyly.

"*Onkel* Levi," she said softly, her cheeks pink with excitement.

Levi smiled, crouching down to her level. "*Gude daag*, Anna. You've grown so much since I last saw you." He glanced at Eli, who was half hiding behind his sister. "And you, too, Eli."

Eli gave a tiny nod, his eyes wide with curiosity.

Rachel put a hand on Levi's shoulder. "Let's get you settled. You must be tired from your journey."

She led him down a hallway to a small comfortable room at the back of the house. The room was simply furnished with a wooden bed, a nightstand, and a chest of drawers. A colorful handmade quilt covered the bed, and a small window afforded a view of the snowy fields.

"I hope this will be all right," Rachel said, her voice holding a hint of concern. "I've tried to make it as comfortable as possible for you."

Levi set his satchel down and turned to her, his heart swelling with gratitude. "It's perfect,

Rachel. *Danki.*"

Rachel smiled, her eyes glistening with unshed tears. "We're so glad you're here, Levi. I know it's been hard, but it will be better now that we are all together."

Levi nodded. "It's *gut* to be with *familye.*"

As Rachel left him to settle in, Levi took a seat on the bed, running his hand contemplatively over the quilt. The faint background sounds of the household drifted around him: Conrad talking to the children, the crackling of the fire, the creaking of the old wooden floorboards. The hums and echoes of everyday family life brought a comforting familiarity, a welcome reminder that he was not alone.

Levi woke the next morning to the sound of soft voices and the clinking of dishes from the kitchen. He dressed and made his way down the hallway, the warm inviting aroma of breakfast drawing him in. He entered upon the scene of his family crowded around the table, the room filled with the comforting bustle of morning activity.

The table was laden with a hearty spread: fresh eggs scrambled with herbs, thick slices of homemade bread, butter, jars of jam and preserves, and a generous plate of crispy bacon. There was also a steaming pot of oatmeal, topped with a mix of dried fruit and honey. Rachel moved gracefully between the stove and the table, placing a fresh batch of pancakes in the center.

"*Gude mariye,* Levi," Rachel greeted with a warm smile. "*Kumm,* sit down and join us."

Levi took a seat next to Eli, who, like his dad and sister, was already busy dishing up his breakfast. Anna sat across from him, her brow furrowed as she argued with her brother over the last piece of bacon.

"I had it first!" Anna insisted, her voice rising.

"*Nee*, you didn't!" Eli shot back, brushing her outstretched hand aside and reaching for the bacon.

Conrad, seated at the head of the table, gently intervened. "Anna, Eli, that's enough. There's plenty of food for everyone. Share, please."

Both children pouted but obeyed, splitting the bacon between them. Levi couldn't help but smile at the familiar sibling rivalry, a small reminder of simpler times.

Rachel poured Levi a cup of coffee and sat down beside him. "What are your plans for today, Levi?"

Levi took a sip of the hot coffee, savoring its warmth. "I thought I might explore the town a bit and get to know Willowvale better."

Rachel nodded, her eyes twinkling with approval. "That sounds like a *gut* idea."

"I thought I might stop in at the bakery," Levi added casually.

"The bakery?" parroted Rachel.

"Mmm," Levi confirmed, taking another sip of coffee. "I met a *maedel* who works there."

"*Ach*," replied Rachel, her eyebrows raised as she and Conrad exchanged a knowing look.

Levi noticed but chose to ignore it, focusing instead on buttering his bread. The truth was that he hadn't been able to stop thinking about Hannah since their chance meeting.

After breakfast, Levi bundled up against the cold, pulling on his coat, hat, and gloves. The winter air was brisk, but the sky was clear, the promise of a bright day ahead.

He sauntered unhurriedly through the village of Willowvale, feeling the curious glances of the townsfolk on him as he passed by. He nodded politely to those he met, sensing their inquisitiveness about the newcomer. The village was abustle with morning activity— children heading to school and men and women starting their daily chores. The sociability of the community was evident in their warm smiles and greetings, which made Levi feel both welcomed and slightly self-conscious.

He approached the bakery, his heart rate accelerating in anticipation. The familiar wooden sign above the entrance swung gently as he opened the door, and the inviting aroma of fresh bread and pastries elicited salivation despite his hearty breakfast. Pausing for a moment's resolve, he pushed the door open wider and stepped inside.

The bakery's warmth enveloped him instantly, a comforting contrast to the chilly air outside. However, his stomach sank with disappointment when he didn't see Hannah behind the counter. Instead, an older woman with kind eyes and a hospitable smile greeted him.

"*Gude mariye,*" she said warmly. "What can I get for you today?"

Levi hesitated and smiled politely. "I was hoping for some of the oatmeal molasses cookies," he answered.

The woman nodded, turning to box up the requested cookies. "They're a favorite around here," she commented conversationally, her voice warm and friendly. "Hannah usually makes them. She's out running an errand but should be back soon."

Though Levi's heart lifted at the mention of Hannah, he tried to keep his cool. As the woman finished boxing up the cookies, the bell above the door jingled, signaling someone's arrival.

Levi turned, his breath catching as he saw Hannah walk in, her cheeks flushed from the cold. She looked surprised but delighted to see him, her eyes lighting up with that familiar sparkle.

"Levi!" she exclaimed, a smile spreading across her face. "I didn't expect to see you here so soon."

Warm pleasure at her greeting washed over Levi. "*Gude daag*, Hannah. I couldn't resist coming in to try those famous oatmeal molasses cookies you mentioned."

Hannah laughed, the joyful sound

reverberating through the bakery. "Well, I'm glad you did. I hope you enjoy them." She moved behind the counter, her presence bringing extra warmth to the cozy atmosphere.

The older woman handed Levi the box of cookies with a knowing smile. "Here you go, young man. Enjoy."

Levi thanked her and turned back to Hannah, feeling a sense of ease and contentment that had been missing from his life for so long. "How's your morning been?"

"Busy," Hannah replied, her cheeks still pink from the wintry chill. "But it's always *gut* to be back in the warmth of the bakery."

Levi nodded, his eyes never leaving hers. "It certainly is a cozy place. I can see why you love it here."

Hannah's smile softened, and joy lit her features. "It is special, isn't it? There's something about this town that just feels like home."

As they chatted, he found himself opening up more about his plans to explore Willowvale and get to know the community better. Hannah listened with genuine interest, her presence comforting and reassuring.

"Why don't you show him around, Hannah,

liewi?" Mrs. Bontrager suggested.

"Are you sure?" asked Hannah.

Mrs. Bontrager nodded. "It's quiet here this morning, and Levi could use a local to show him all the *gut* spots."

Hannah turned to Levi. "What do you think?"

"I think I could use a guide," Levi affirmed.

Hannah beamed. "All right," she said. "Let's go."

Hannah knowledgeably and enthusiastically pointed out various landmarks as they walked down the snow-dusted street. As they approached the general store, a robust man with a graying beard and a friendly smile greeted them. "*Ach*, you must be the new fellow I've been hearing about," he said, extending a hand. "Levi, isn't it?"

Levi shook his hand warmly. "*Ya*, that's right, Mr...."

"Smoker," he said. "Noah Smoker."

"Well, it's nice to meet you, Mr. Smoker."

As they continued their walk, Hannah introduced Levi to more townsfolk, with him experiencing each encounter as filled with genuine warmth and interest. They met Mrs.

Ebersole, tending to her garden even in the snow, and the blacksmith, Samuel Flaud, whose powerful frame and booming laugh belied his gentle nature.

Hannah led him past the schoolhouse. As they walked further, Hannah turned to him.

"So, what was your old town like?"

"It had more modern conveniences," he admitted. "Some homes had generators and electric lights. It was still Amish but a bit more... progressive, I guess you could say."

Hannah smiled, her eyes twinkling with amusement. "My *daed* is the bishop here, and he's very strict about keeping to the traditional ways. No electricity, no phones. He believes in preserving our heritage."

Levi nodded, appreciating the simplicity and authenticity of Willowvale. "It's nice, though."

"I'm glad you think so," she said. "So, Levi Miller, what do you plan to do now that you are in Willowvale?"

Levi looked thoughtful. "I would like to find some work," he answered.

"*Ach*?" Hannah said. "What kind of work?"

"Well my *daed* was a carpenter," he replied. "And I've always enjoyed working with my hands."

"Perhaps you can speak with Mr. Fisher," suggested Hannah. "He's the town's carpenter."

Levi nodded. "So, what about you?" he asked.

"What about me?"

"Have you lived in Willowvale all your life?"

Hannah nodded.

"And do you enjoy working at the bakery?" he asked.

"I do," said Hannah with a wistful smile. "My mother loved to bake, and I suppose being there makes me feel closer to her."

Before Levi could say anything else, he spotted a young man a short distance away with his gaze fixed on them. A pile of books was tucked under his arm.

"Do you know him?" Levi asked, frowning.

Hannah turned, and her shoulders dropped perceptibly.

"Hannah?" said the young man as he approached.

"*Gude daag*, Daniel," Hannah responded politely.

"I was just on my way to return these books to the library. What are you doing out here?"

"I'm showing Levi around town. Levi, this is

Daniel King, a friend of mine. Daniel, this is Levi Miller. He's new in Willowvale."

Levi extended a hand and politely said, "Nice to meet you."

Daniel shook Levi's hand, his grip firm. "Likewise," he said though his eyes remained cool. "What brings you to our town, Levi?"

Levi met Daniel's gaze steadily. "I'm here to stay with my *schweschder*, Rachel Peachey, and her *familye*.

Daniel nodded slowly, looking not entirely convinced. "I see."

Hannah's gaze bounced between the two men, a slight crease on her otherwise smooth brow. "I should get back to the bakery," she interjected. "Mrs. Bontrager will be wondering where I am."

"I'll walk you back," Levi and Daniel both said at the same time.

Hannah laughed lightly, a hint of awkwardness in her smile. "That's very kind of both of you, but I'll be fine. It's just a short walk."

Levi felt a pang of disappointment but nodded. "*Danki* for the tour, Hannah."

Hannah returned his smile, her eyes soft. "*Gaern gschehne*, Levi. I'm sure I'll see you around."

She turned and walked away, leaving Levi and Daniel standing on the sidewalk. The moment she was out of earshot, Daniel turned back to Levi, his expression more guarded as he crossed his arms and assessed Levi, looking him up and down.

"So, how long do you plan on staying in Willowvale?" he asked, his tone casual but with an unmistakable edge.

"Indefinitely," Levi replied evenly, boldly meeting Daniel's gaze. "I like it here."

Daniel nodded slowly, his eyes narrowing slightly. "You should know, Levi, I've known Hannah since we were *kinner*. We're very close."

"*Gut* for you," said Levi with a hint of sarcasm.

Daniel stepped closer, his posture not too subtly challenging. "We look out for each other here, and we're very protective of our own. I just wanted to make sure you understand that."

"Loud and clear," Levi enunciated, his unwavering gaze still fixed on Daniel.

"Well, *gut*," Daniel volleyed, taking a step back. "Just so we are clear."

Levi said nothing further.

"See you around, Levi."

Without another word, Daniel turned and walked away. Levi got the distinct feeling that he'd already, albeit unintentionally, made an enemy.

Chapter Three

Mary sat at the dinner table, her hands resting limply in her lap. The clinking of cutlery and the sound of voices sounded distant and muffled to her. Timothy and Ruth, Isaac's parents, were there for dinner, their presence a painful reminder of the normalcy that had once been a part of her life.

"So, have you two thought about your plans for *Grischtdaag*?" Timothy asked, his voice warm and cheerful. "It's only a few weeks away."

Mary stared at her plate, the food untouched. The smell of roasted chicken, fresh bread, and steamed vegetables wafted up, churning her stomach. She hadn't eaten properly in days, the grief consuming her appetite and leaving her hollow and empty. She could feel Isaac's eyes on her but couldn't bring herself to meet his gaze.

"We were thinking maybe you could *kumm* to our place this year," Ruth continued, her tone inviting. "We can all be together to support each other. What do you think, Mary?"

Mary remained silent.

"Well, I've been dreaming of Mary's apple pie," Timothy added emphatically. "We'd love to have your apple pie at the table."

Again, Mary said nothing.

"Mary—" Isaac began.

"The chicken is *appeditlich*, Mary," Ruth interjected, effectively cutting him off. "You've really outdone yourself."

Mary gave a faint nod, her lowered gaze fixed on her untouched plate. "*Danki*," she murmured, the words scraping against her throat.

"The school *Grischtdaag* program is coming up," Ruth segued. "Maybe we can all go together."

"Maybe," Isaac agreed.

Suddenly Mary felt the walls closing in, the room growing smaller and the air thicker. She couldn't breathe.

"Mary, are you all right?" Isaac asked softly, his concern breaking through her foggy state.

His words were the final straw. She couldn't

take it anymore, the conversation, the pretense of normalcy—it was all too much. Abruptly, she stood, the chair scraping loudly against the floor. The sudden movement drew everyone's attention, and the room fell silent.

"I...I need some air," she stammered, her voice trembling. Without waiting for a response, she turned and fled the room, her footsteps echoing in the quiet.

The cold night air hit her like a shock as she stepped outside, but it was a welcome relief. She wrapped her arms around her torso, trying to control her breathing and calm her racing heart. The stars above glittered coldly, indifferent to her pain. She walked a few steps, then leaned against the side of the house, taking deep, shaky breaths.

As she stood there, her thoughts drifted back to the previous Christmas—when Grace was still alive. The memory was so vivid and so painful. She could almost hear Grace's laughter and see her bright eyes sparkling with excitement as she tore into her presents.

They had spent the entire day together, the house filled with joy and warmth. Grace had insisted on helping Mary make the Christmas cookies. Her tiny hands patted out the dough with such concentration. Flour had ended up everywhere—on the floor, on their faces, even in Grace's hair. They had laughed so hard, and Mary remembered thinking how perfect everything felt.

Grace had been especially excited about the wooden dollhouse Isaac made for her. She had spent hours playing with it, her imagination creating elaborate stories for her little wooden figurines. Mary could still hear her daughter's sweet voice chattering happily as she arranged the tiny furniture and spoke animatedly for her characters.

Later, they had all gathered around the table to share Christmas dinner. Timothy and Ruth were there, too, their laughter and stories filling the room. But Grace had been the light of the evening, her presence making everything brighter, more enchanting.

The stark contrast between that Christmas and the present moment was almost too much to bear. The thought of facing another holiday without Grace was salt in a wound that seemed to intensify with each passing day. Tears welled up in Mary's eyes, and she pressed her hands to her face in an attempt to hold back the sobs that threatened to escape.

She felt so alone, even with Isaac and his parents a few steps away. The grief of losing Grace had created a chasm between her and the rest of the world, a chasm she didn't know how to cross. She wanted to scream, to cry, to lash out, but all she could do was stand there, her body shaking with silent sobs.

She heard the door open and close softly behind her but didn't turn, knowing it was Isaac. She could feel his presence and his concern, but she couldn't face him.

"Mary," he said quietly, his voice raw with pain. "Please *kumm* back inside."

She shook her head, unable to speak.

"My *eldre* are worried about you. We all are."

"I'm sorry," Mary whispered.

"You don't need to be sorry," Isaac soothed, the porch creaking under his weight as he took a step forward. "Just let us help you—"

"How?" Mary snapped, pivoting to face him. "Can you bring our *dochder* back?"

Isaac's shoulders fell as he stepped closer, but he didn't touch her. "I miss her, too, Mary," he said, his voice breaking. "Every day, I miss her.

But we have to find a way to live. For her and for us."

Mary let out a choked sob, the sound finally escaping her lips. "I don't know how," she whispered despairingly. "I don't know how to live without her."

Isaac wordlessly reached for her hand, but she stepped back out of reach.

"You should go back inside," she said as she turned away.

Isaac hesitated briefly; then Mary heard the door open and the soft click of the latch as it closed.

After Timothy and Ruth left, the house fell into a thick, heavy silence. As Isaac moved about in the kitchen cleaning up the remnants of dinner, Mary sat at the table for a while, staring blankly at the untouched food on her plate. The echoes of Timothy and Ruth's laughter still rang in her ears, mingling cruelly with her memories of Grace's joyful laughter from her last Christmas.

Finally, Isaac finished tidying up and retreated to his workshop, the familiar sound of his footsteps disappearing out the door. Mary watched him go, a pang of guilt and longing choking her. She wanted to follow him, to talk to him, to somehow bridge the chasm that had grown between them. But what could she say? How could words possibly convey the depth of her sorrow and her helplessness?

At that moment, Mary felt the pull toward Grace's room. It was a sanctuary of sorts, a place where she could still feel close to her daughter. She paced down the hall, her footsteps slow and deliberate, as if each step brought her closer to the memories that both comforted and tormented her.

Mary walked across the room to the dollhouse and knelt down beside it, her fingers trembling as she reached out to touch the tiny wooden furniture. Each piece was a work of art, crafted with love and care. She picked up a small chair, reverently running her fingers over the smooth wood, remembering the joy on Grace's face when she first saw it.

She gently rearranged the miniature furniture, her mind drifting back to the countless hours Grace had spent playing there, her sweet voice narrating the lives of the little wooden figurines. As she moved a small-scale bed into place, tears welled up in Mary's eyes. She missed Grace with an almost unbearable intensity, a pain that was sharp and constant. The memories were a double-edged sword, offering comfort yet deepening the sense of loss.

Mary knew that Isaac was hurting, too. She had seen the pain in his eyes, the way his shoulders sagged. He sought refuge in his workshop, pouring his sorrow into the wood he shaped, but the distance between the two of them widened with each passing day.

Mary stood up slowly, her gaze lingering on the dollhouse one last time before she turned away. She retraced her steps down the hall and out of the house, pausing outside Isaac's workshop. The door was closed, the faint sounds of his tools the only indication of his presence.

Mary placed her hand on the door, her heart heavy with longing. She wanted to open it, to step inside and be with him, but she felt paralyzed by her own grief. Instead, she leaned against the door, her tears flowing freely. She whispered a silent prayer for the strength to find her way back to him, to find a way through the darkness that enveloped them both.

∞ ∞ ∞

The next day found Mary sitting in the quiet kitchen, staring at the table. She hadn't seen Isaac that morning; he had slept in his workshop. A knock at the door registered through her hazy thoughts and she mechanically rose and opened it to find Hannah standing there, her cheeks flushed from the cold and a hopeful smile on her face.

"*Gude mariye*, Mary," Hannah said brightly. "I thought maybe we could take a walk. It's a beautiful day."

Mary shook her head, feeling a wave of exhaustion at the mere thought. "I don't know, Hannah. I'm just so tired."

Hannah stepped closer, her eyes filled with gentle insistence. "Just a short walk. It'll be *gut* for you, really."

Reluctantly, Mary agreed. She wrapped herself in her warmest coat, donning her gloves and hat. They stepped outside into the cool, crisp air, the sky a clear, bright blue. At first, they walked in silence, Mary's steps heavy and slow, but as they continued, she found herself breathing a little easier. The cold air was invigorating, and despite her initial reticence, she did indeed feel better from being outside.

Hannah led them to the small park at the village edge, a peaceful spot, the trees dusted with snow and the ground a virgin white. Hannah removed her scarf and dusted the snow off a bench before sitting down. Mary hesitated, then joined her, the cold seeping through her coat as she sat.

They sat in companionable silence for a while, and Mary's thoughts drifted back to the times she had brought Grace to the park. She could almost hear Grace's laughter, see her tiny footprints in the snow, and feel the warmth of her little hand in hers.

Just then, a few children arrived at the park, their laughter ringing out as they romped in the snow. Mary watched them, her heart squeezing in her chest. She could see her little Grace in every joyful face, every burst of laughter. A little girl in a red coat ran past, her giggles echoing in the crisp air, and Mary's breath caught in her throat. The girl's auburn curls bounced with each step, much as Grace's had. She was about the same age, and her eyes sparkled with the same innocent delight. Mary sat as stock-still as a statue as she watched the girl build a small snowman, her mitten-clad hands clumsy but determined as she patted the snow into shape.

The other children joined in, adding sticks for arms and a scarf around the snowman's neck. Their laughter intensified and grew more exuberant, and Mary could almost hear Grace's voice among them, a phantom echo of the past. Grace had loved the snow; her cheeks would be rosy with excitement and her eyes bright with joy whenever she raced happily up a snowy bank and slid down, laughing in gleeful abandon. Mary's vision blurred with tears at the memories, distorting the scene before her.

A small boy, his face red from the cold, called out to the girl, and she turned, her laughter echoing through the park. The sound was a knife to Mary's heart, sharp and painful. She pressed her hand to her mouth, trying to stifle the sobs that threatened to escape.

Hannah, sensing Mary's distress, placed a gentle hand on her arm. "Mary, are you all right?"

she asked softly.

Mary shook her head, unable to speak. The pain was too raw, too overwhelming. She stood abruptly, her entire body trembling. "I need to go home," she managed, her voice breaking.

Hannah nodded, understanding in her eyes. "*Ach*, of course, Mary. Let's go."

As they walked back to Mary's house, the sounds of the children's laughter followed them, a haunting reminder of what Mary had lost. Each step felt heavy; her grief pressing down on her like a physical weight. She felt as though she were walking through a dream, the world around her muted and distant.

When they reached her home, Mary opened the front door and then turned to Hannah, her emotions raw and close to the surface. "I'm sorry, Hannah," she choked. "I know you're trying to help, but it's just too hard. I can't do this."

Hannah reached out, her eyes filled with sympathy and regret. "I'm so sorry, Mary. I didn't mean to upset you—"

Mary shook her head, her tears spilling over and sliding down her cheeks. "I think it's best if you leave. I need to be alone."

Hannah hesitated, then nodded, stepping

back. Mary watched her go. She closed the door behind her and leaned against it as the dam wall gave way and the tears flowed freely. She had pushed Hannah away, and now the silence of the house felt even more oppressive. But she couldn't handle the outside world yet. She needed to be alone with her grief and to find a way through the darkness on her own terms.

Chapter Four

The familiar smell of sawdust and varnish surrounded Isaac like a comforting blanket as he stood in his workshop. The rhythmic sound of his hand planer smoothing a piece of oak was calming, almost meditative. The place had become his sanctuary, a haven where he could lose himself in the work and for a little while each day, forget the ache in his heart.

His perfectly appointed workshop was a tribute to the generations of carpenters from whom he had learned his craft. There were wooden shelves along one wall that held neatly organized jars of nails, screws, and various small pieces of hardware. A large cabinet stood in the corner, its doors open to reveal the assortment of stains, varnishes, and paints used to add final touches to the wooden creations assembled by his hands. The walls were covered with hand-drawn plans and sketches, some faded with age, others more recent, showcasing designs for all his carpentry projects from simple chairs to intricate dollhouses.

Isaac loved his space. It represented both familiarity and purpose, filled with the rich, earthy aroma of freshly cut wood.

He paused, wiping the sweat from his brow. He was hot despite the cold winter air outside. His thoughts drifted to dinner the previous evening and the way Mary had abruptly left the table. The image of her standing outside in the cold, her shoulders wracked with silent sobs, haunted him. He was so worried about her. Mary had always been the strong one, her faith an anchor in many of life's storms. But now, she seemed adrift, her confidence and trust in God shaken by the loss of their daughter.

Isaac was at his wit's end about how to help her. He felt as if he was failing his dear Mary, unable to bridge the canyon that had grown between them since Grace's death. Isaac missed their daughter every day. The ache of her absence was constant. But his faith had been his anchor, God, his lifeline. He couldn't imagine facing such darkness without God.

He ran a hand through his hair, frustration and helplessness welling up inside him. How could he help Mary find her faith again? How could he support her when she seemed to be clinging to an iceberg that was slipping further away from him, refusing to reach out and grasp his hand? He felt as though they would soon be separated by so great a distance that he wouldn't be able to reach her and it would be too late.

Isaac picked up a small unfinished toy he had been working on—a wooden horse, meant for Grace. He had started it back when their lives were filled with the simple joys of parenthood. Now, it was a painful reminder of all they lost. He set it down with a sigh, his fingers tracing the smooth lines of the wood.

He remembered fondly the joy in Grace's eyes when she played with the toys he made for her. She had loved spending time in the workshop with him, her contagious childish laughter filling the space as she tried to mimic his actions with her own small tools.

The sound of the front door opening and

closing reached him, and he knew Mary had returned from her walk with Hannah. He hoped the outing did her some good, but a part of him feared that it might only have served to remind her of what she had lost. He wanted to go to her, to offer comfort, but he didn't know what to say. Words felt inadequate in the face of such profound grief.

He continued his work, the chisel biting into the wood with each measured stroke. As he worked, he prayed silently, asking God for the strength to support Mary, to find a way to heal their fractured relationship. He prayed for guidance and that they would find their way back to each other.

Isaac's thoughts drifted back to the early days of their marriage when their love had been a source of unshakable strength. They had faced challenges before but nothing so significant as losing a child. He didn't know how to fix things now that their Grace was gone. The foundation of their life together had fragmented, and it felt as if he was groping in the dark as he tried to piece the shards back together.

He set down the chisel and rubbed his eyes, the cumulative weariness of the past months hitting him. He loved Mary deeply, but he felt powerless to help her. He could see the pain in her eyes, and the heaviness with which she conducted herself broke his heart. He longed to reach out to her, to find the right words that would bring them closer, but the distance between them seemed insurmountable.

A knock at the door interrupted him just then. He set the tool down and opened the door to find a young man standing there. His eyes held a look of determination despite the clear signs of recent hardship etched on his face.

"*Gude daag,*" he said, extending his hand. "I'm Levi Miller. I hope I'm not interrupting."

Isaac wiped his hands on a rag and shook Levi's hand firmly. "Isaac Fisher. It's no trouble at all. What can I do for you?"

Levi looked around the workshop, taking in the tools and the half-finished projects. "I'm looking for work," he said, getting straight to the point. "Hannah Weaver mentioned you might need some help."

Isaac nodded. "Do you have any experience with carpentry?"

Levi hesitated for a moment before replying. "My *vadder* was a carpenter. I helped him a lot growing up. But I have to admit, you don't have the more modern equipment he had in his workshop."

Isaac frowned at the mention of modern equipment, then sighed. He understood the temptation and convenience of modern tools, but they had always stuck to traditional methods in Willowvale. "We do things a bit differently here," he said carefully. "We believe in preserving our ways, keeping things simple and grounded in tradition."

Levi nodded thoughtfully. "I understand. I'm willing to learn and adapt. I just want to work and keep busy. Truthfully, I need something to keep my hands and mind occupied."

Isaac studied Levi for a moment, perceiving the sincerity and desperation in his eyes. Isaac was used to working alone and liked his solitude. Still, he could use the help, especially with Christmas coming and the toy orders piling up.

"All right, Levi. I'm under the whip with *Grischtdaag* orders, especially toys, so I could use an extra pair of hands. I'll give you a trial."

Levi's face brightened with relief and gratitude. "*Danki*," he said. I won't let you down."

Isaac led Levi deeper into the workshop,

explaining the various tasks he had lined up. As they moved through the space, Isaac warmed to the idea of having Levi around and how his assistance might bring some much-needed energy and support.

"Let's start with something simple," Isaac determined, handing Levi a piece of sandpaper and a wooden toy car that needed smoothing. "I need this car finished by the end of the day. Give it a *gut* sanding, and then we'll move on to painting it."

Levi took the sandpaper and the toy car and got started right away, his movements deliberate and focused. Isaac observed him for a moment, then returned to his own work, feeling a small spark of hope. Perhaps having Levi around would be good for all of them.

As they worked side by side, the silence was comfortable, punctuated only by the sounds of their tools.

After a while, Levi spoke up, breaking the silence. "Mr. Fisher, if you don't mind me asking, how did you become the town carpenter?"

Isaac paused, considering the question. "It's been in my *familye* for generations. My *vadder* taught me, just as his *vadder* taught him.

Working with wood has always been a part of my life. It's more than just a job; it's a way of connecting with the past and creating something lasting."

Levi nodded, understanding what Isaac was saying on a deeper level and not merely at face value. The two men continued their work, the rhythm of their tasks generating a sense of quiet calmness in the workshop. The steady rasp of sandpaper smoothed rough edges, the sharp, precise clicks of chisels carved out delicate details, and the rhythmic thud of a mallet striking wood added a rhythmic bass tone in the background. Occasionally, the gentle hum of a hand-cranked lathe would join the mix, its soft whir adding a soothing undertone. The comforting smells of sawdust and freshly cut wood permeated the air. The aromas of pine and cedar were particularly pungent, mingling with the faint hint of varnish and oil.

Every now and then, Isaac glanced across at Levi. As the midday sun began to filter in through the small-paned windows, casting a warm golden hue across the sawdust-speckled floor, Isaac glanced across at the clock on the wall.

"It's about lunchtime," he commented. "How about we take a break and head to the house for something to eat?"

Levi nodded, setting down the sandpaper and the toy car. "Sounds *gut* to me."

They left the workshop and made their way toward the house. As they approached, they came upon Hannah standing outside with a basket in her hands. She looked up, her eyes widening in surprise at seeing Levi.

"Levi! What are you doing here?" she asked, a smile spreading across her face.

Levi grinned back at her. "I took your advice. Mr. Fisher was kind enough to give me a chance."

Isaac stepped forward. "Hannah," he said. "What brings you by?"

Hannah glanced at the basket in her hands, then back up at Isaac. "I...I think I upset Mary earlier," she confessed. "We went for a walk and there were some *kinner* in the park..."

Her voice trailed off as she glanced at Levi.

"I just wanted to bring her something from the bakery to apologize."

Isaac nodded, valuing her thoughtfulness. "That's kind of you," he said appreciatively. Why don't you *kumm* inside with us? We were just about to have lunch."

Hannah hesitated for a moment, then nodded.

Isaac led the way into the house, holding the door open for Levi and Hannah. The warmth of the home enfolded them as they stepped inside, the tantalizing aroma of freshly baked bread and soup filling the air.

Mary, setting the table in the kitchen, looked up, surprised to see Hannah and Levi with Isaac. Her eyes flickered to the basket in Hannah's hands, then back to Isaac.

"Hannah brought us something from the bakery," Isaac explained gently. "She wanted to apologize for earlier."

Hannah stepped forward, her expression sincere. "Mary, I'm so sorry if I upset you," she said, handing her the basket. "I hope you can forgive me."

Mary's gaze softened, and she nodded. "That's very kind of you," she said. "But unnecessary; you did nothing wrong."

Hannah smiled tightly.

"And who is this?" Mary asked, looking at Levi.

"Levi Miller. It's nice to meet you, Mrs.

Fisher."

"Levi is going to be helping me in the workshop," Isaac clarified.

Mary raised her eyebrows but said nothing.

They all sat down at the table and bowed their heads in silent prayer before the meal. As they ate, Mary kept her head down and gaze averted, her focus entirely on her plate.

"How was your morning, Mary?" asked Isaac.

"Fine," Mary said automatically without looking up.

Isaac nodded.

"So, Levi," Hannah said, breaking the uncomfortable silence. "How are you settling into Willowvale?"

"Very well," Levi replied, his eyes shining. "I've met some really nice people."

Hannah flushed. "I'm glad your stay is off to a good start."

"I was thinking of stopping by the bakery this afternoon," Levi continued. "My *niess* and *neffyu* devoured those oatmeal molasses cookies, and I promised I would get some more."

"Sure," said Hannah, smiling.

Isaac looked between Levi and Hannah; the connection between the two was clear as day.

The manner in which they looked at each other and the ease and warmth between them struck a chord deep within Isaac. It reminded him of the early days of his relationship with Mary, a time filled with hope and endless possibilities. They had met at a barn raising, an event that brought the entire community together. Isaac had been working alongside the other men, lifting beams and hammering nails, when he first laid eyes on Mary. She was helping to prepare the midday meal, her light brown hair tucked neatly under her prayer *kapp*, her delicate features accentuated by the soft light of the afternoon sun.

Their eyes had met across the busy yard, and a jolt of electricity shot through Isaac. Mary had smiled shyly, her hazel eyes twinkling with curiosity. Isaac, usually confident, had found himself nervous and tongue-tied when he made his way over to her during the lunch break.

"*Gude daag*," he'd said, his voice catching slightly. "I'm Isaac. I've seen you around, but I don't think we've ever really talked."

Mary had looked up from her task of setting out bread and cheese, her cheeks flushing a delicate pink. "I'm Mary. It's *gut* to finally meet you properly, Isaac."

They had talked for the rest of the lunch break, finding common ground in their shared faith and love for their community. Isaac was struck by Mary's kindness and gentle spirit, qualities that seemed to shine through in everything she did. Her laughter was like music, light and infectious, and Isaac found himself wanting to hear it again and again.

Over the next few months, they saw each other frequently at community events and church services. Isaac would always find an excuse to be near her, whether it was helping with a chore or simply walking her home after a gathering. Their conversations grew longer and more personal, each one deepening the bond between them.

One evening, as they walked home from a quilting bee, Isaac had gathered the courage to take Mary's hand. Her fingers were warm and soft in his, and she had looked up at him.

"Mary," he had said, his voice steady despite the butterflies in his stomach. "I know we haven't known each other for long, but I feel like I've known you forever. You're the kindest, most *wunderbaar* person I've ever met. I can't imagine my life without you in it."

Mary had squeezed his hand, her eyes shining with unshed tears. "I feel the same way, Isaac. I've been waiting for you to say that."

Their courtship was a whirlwind of stolen glances, private smiles, and shared times that were both thrilling and tender. Isaac remembered the night he had asked Mary to marry him, taking her to the small hill overlooking the fields where they often walked. He had carved their initials into the trunk of a tree, promising to add the names of their children as they grew old together.

Mary had said yes, her eyes filled with love and joy. They had kissed under the stars, their future stretching out before them like a smooth as-yet-untrodden beach. Those early days were a time of pure happiness, unmarred by the hardships that would come later.

Watching Levi and Hannah filled Isaac with a bittersweet ache; the way they behaved toward each other reminded him of those precious early days with Mary, a time when everything seemed possible. He glanced at Mary, whose head remained dipped, lost in her own world of grief. Isaac yearned to reach out to her, to find a way back to the closeness they had once shared.

As the afternoon wore on, the bright light filtering through the workshop windows began to fade into the shadowy hues of early evening. Isaac glanced up from his work and looked at Levi, who was diligently sanding another toy car. The younger man had shown a remarkable dedication and a willingness to learn, and Isaac appreciated his quiet presence.

Isaac walked over to where Levi was working and assessed the toy car. The edges were smooth, and the surface had a fine finish that showed Levi's careful attention to detail. Isaac nodded approvingly.

"You've done fine work, Levi," Isaac said, his voice sincere.

"*Danki*," said Levi, a smile tugging at the corners of his lips.

Isaac set the toy car aside and clapped Levi on the shoulder. "I think that's enough for today. Why don't you head home and get some rest?"

Levi wiped his hands on a rag and nodded.

"All right."

"I'll see you right after breakfast, okay? There's plenty more to do before *Grischtdaag*."

"Sure," Levi agreed, gathering his things and making his way to the door.

As he left, he turned back and gave Isaac a grateful nod. *"Gude nacht,"* he said. "See you tomorrow."

"Gude nacht, Levi," Isaac replied, watching him go. He stood for a moment listening to the quiet sounds of the evening settling in. The workshop felt a little emptier without Levi's presence, but it also felt like a place of progress, of moving forward.

Isaac then returned to his workbench, organizing his tools and tidying up the workspace before he, too, would head home. He was lost in thought when he heard footsteps approaching. Turning, he was surprised to find Bishop Weaver standing in the doorway.

Bishop Weaver was a tall man with a powerful, imposing presence. His silver hair and neatly trimmed beard gave him an air of wisdom and authority, and his deep blue eyes were kind but piercing, seeming to look into the very soul of a person. He wore the traditional plain black suit and broad-brimmed hat of their community, his posture straight and unwavering.

"Bishop Weaver," Isaac said by way of greeting, setting down his broom and wiping his hands on his apron. "This is a surprise."

The Bishop stepped into the workshop, his gaze taking in the neatly organized tools and the projects in various stages of completion. "I hope I'm not intruding, Isaac. I was on my way home, and thought I'd stop in to see how you and Mary are doing."

Isaac felt a pang of guilt; they hadn't been to church as much of late, and he knew their absence had not gone unnoticed.

"*Nee*, you're not intruding at all. It's *gut* to see you."

Bishop Weaver nodded, his eyes softening. "I've been concerned about you both. I know this has been a difficult time."

Isaac sighed, leaning against his workbench. "It has been. Mary...she's struggling. I don't like to leave her alone, and she hasn't felt up to going to church."

The bishop stepped closer, placing a hand on Isaac's shoulder. "It's understandable, Isaac. Grief can be a heavy burden to bear. But remember, the church is a community, a *familye*. We are here to support you both."

Isaac nodded, swallowing past the lump forming in his throat. "I know. It's just…it's hard to see her like this. I don't know how to help her."

Bishop Weaver's eyes were filled with empathy. "Sometimes, the best way to help is simply to be there. To listen and to pray. *Gott's* love and guidance are always with us, even in the darkest times."

Isaac looked down, his voice quiet. "I pray every day, but honestly it feels like we're drifting further apart. I don't want to lose her, too," he added, his voice a hoarse whisper.

The bishop squeezed his shoulder gently. "You won't lose her, Isaac. Your love for each other and your faith in *Gott* are strong. Trust in *Gott*'s plan, even when it's hard to see. And don't be afraid to lean on your *gmay*. We are here for you."

Isaac looked up, meeting the bishop's steady gaze. "*Danki*, Bishop Weaver. Your words mean a lot. I'll try to remember that."

The bishop gave a small reassuring smile. "It's natural to feel lost sometimes. But *Gott* is always with us, guiding us through our trials.

Lean on Him and on each other."

Isaac nodded.

The bishop gave his shoulder one last supportive squeeze before stepping back. "Take care, Isaac. I hope we will see you and Mary soon."

Bishop Weaver turned to go, leaving Isaac alone again. He finished packing away his tools and wiped down the tables before closing up the workshop and heading to the house. As he approached the back door, he paused. Through the small window, he caught sight of Mary sitting alone at the table, tears streaming down her face. His heart ached at the sight. What could he say to make things better? What could he do? He just didn't know. But he paused and prayed that in time, the answers would come to him and he would finally be able to be the husband Mary needed to find her peace again.

Chapter Five

Hannah stood outside the Fisher house, taking a deep breath before knocking purposefully on the door. After their walk to the park the previous day, Hannah was more determined to do whatever she could to help.

Mary opened the door; her eyes were red from crying, but she offered a small polite smile.

"Hannah," she breathed softly.

"*Gude daag*, Mary," said Hannah. "I was hoping you might join me at the bakery today. Mrs. Bontrager has gone to visit her *soh*, so it will just be me there."

Mary hesitated, her eyes dropping to the floor. "*Ach,* I don't know, Hannah. I'm not sure I'm up for it."

"Perhaps just for a little while," Hannah coaxed. "Sometimes keeping busy can be a *gut* distraction. And we don't have to talk if you don't want to."

Mary chewed her bottom lip and, after a moment, nodded. "All right. I'll *kumm* with you. Let me just get dressed."

They walked to the bakery together, the crisp invigorating morning air filling their lungs. The streets were quiet. Hannah glanced at Mary now and again, whose gaze was fixed ahead, her eyes distant.

As they entered the bakery, Hannah handed Mary an apron and guided her to the kitchen.

"We need to make some Amish friendship bread," Hannah instructed, smiling gently. "It's always been a favorite around here."

Hannah walked over to the counter and removed the risen dough from its bowl. She pulled it into two pieces and handed one to Mary. Hannah began to roll out her piece of dough on the table, alternating between stretching it out and folding it over.

Mary followed her lead, hesitantly pressing her hands into the soft dough. They worked in silence for a few minutes, the steady motion of kneading providing a calming atmosphere.

Hannah glanced at Mary, then said gently, "Grace loved to bake, didn't she?"

Mary's hands stilled, but then she nodded. "She did. She always wanted to help in the kitchen—even if it meant making a mess."

Hannah smiled. "I remember her coming into the bakery. She was always full of questions."

Mary's lips curved into a faint smile. "She used to say she was going to open her own bakery one day."

Hannah's eyes sparkled with warmth. "She would have been a *gut* baker. She had such a bright spirit."

Mary nodded. "*Ya*, she would have," she agreed, the corners of her mouth turning down.

"What else did she like to do?" Hannah prompted.

Mary opened her mouth, then closed it again as she lowered her gaze.

"It's okay to talk about her," Hannah encouraged softly. "It's nice to remember the happy times."

Mary looked up, her eyes filled with tears. "I want to talk about her, but it hurts to remember.

Every time I think about her, my heart shatters like I'm losing her all over again."

Hannah stepped closer, placing a comforting hand on Mary's arm. "I know it's hard. Grief is like that. But reminiscing keeps her memory alive. And it helps you heal—even if it doesn't feel that way right now."

Mary took a shuddering breath, her tears spilling over. "I miss her so much," she said, her voice barely a whisper. "She was my whole world."

"I know," Hannah said compassionately. "But she would want you to remember her as she was, as the bright and kind little *maedel* you loved and raised."

Mary nodded, exhaling shakily.

"And she would want you to *live*," Hannah continued. "To do the things she loved to do, to honor her memory."

A lone tear trickled down Mary's cheek, and Hannah reached into her pocket to remove a small white handkerchief, which she handed to Mary.

"We should get back to it," Mary said in a tight voice. "Before I collapse completely."

Hannah smiled softly, and the kitchen fell

silent for a while, the rhythm of kneading dough becoming a shared, almost reflective act.

After they finished kneading, they shaped the loaves by placing them into the prepared pans.

Hannah slid the pans into the oven, turning to Mary with a warm smile. "Now that the bread is baking, how about we make some apple fritters?"

Mary nodded.

Hannah gathered the ingredients, setting them out on the counter.

"First, we need to prepare the filling," said Hannah, slicing the apples into thin pieces. "We'll cook them down with some sugar and cinnamon until they're nice and soft."

Mary watched as Hannah placed the apple slices in a pot, adding a generous amount of sugar and a sprinkle of cinnamon. The mixture sizzled softly as it began to cook, filling the air with a sweet, spicy aroma.

While the apples simmered, they prepared the dough. Hannah measured out the flour, yeast, and a pinch of salt, combining them in a large bowl. She added warm milk, melted butter, and a few beaten eggs, stirring until the dough came together in a smooth elastic ball.

"Now, we let this rise for a bit," Hannah said as she covered the bowl with a clean cloth. "In the meantime, let's check on the apples."

The apple filling was bubbling gently, the slices turning soft and translucent. Hannah stirred the mixture, inhaling the comforting scent. "This is coming along nicely."

Once the dough had risen, they turned it out onto a floured surface and began to roll it out into a thin sheet. Hannah showed Mary how to cut the dough into squares, each one destined to be filled with the sweet apple filling.

"Now, for the fun part," Hannah announced with a smile. She spooned a small amount of the apple filling onto each square of dough, then carefully folded the edges over, sealing them into little pockets.

Mary followed suit, her movements growing more confident with each pastry. Once they had finished folding the pockets, Hannah heated a pot of oil, waiting until it was just the right temperature. She gently lowered a few of the apple-filled dough pockets into the hot oil, watching as they puffed up and turned golden brown. The smell of the frying pastries was irresistible, filling the kitchen with a warm inviting fragrance.

Mary watched, a small smile playing on her lips. "I remember making these with my *maem* when I was just a *maedel*. She always let me have the first one. I'd almost forgotten how to make them."

Hannah smiled, too, carefully lifting the golden pastries out of the oil and placing them on a paper towel to drain. "Well, today you get to have the first one again."

She dusted the warm fritters with powdered sugar and handed one to Mary. Mary took a bite, closing her eyes as the flavor-burst filled her mouth. "This is *appeditlich,* Hannah. Just like I remember."

Hannah felt a sense of satisfaction at seeing Mary find a second's peace in a sweet childhood memory. "I'm glad," she said. Sometimes, it's the little things that help us remember the *gut* times."

After they cleaned up, Hannah looked at Mary and said, "You can *kumm* by anytime, you know. The bakery is always open to you."

Mary smiled softly. "*Danki,* Hannah. If it's all right, I think I will head home now. I'm feeling a little tired."

Hannah nodded in understanding. "Of course, Mary."

Mary doffed her apron and handed it back to Hannah. "*Danki* for being so kind, Hannah. It did help coming here. I do feel a bit better."

Hannah's heart lifted at Mary's words.

She watched as Mary gathered her things and headed for the door. "I'll see you soon," Hannah called.

Mary turned back briefly, her smile clearer this time. "See you soon, Hannah."

As Mary walked down the street headed homeward, Hannah stood in the doorway, watching her. The day had been a small step, but it was a step in the right direction. She prayed that Mary would find her way back from the edge of despair one step at a time and that each step would bring her closer to healing.

Hannah turned from the cool breeze brushing against her face and went back into the bakery, and the warmth of the kitchen and the lingering scent of fresh bread renewed her resolve. She knew it wouldn't be easy, but she was committed to reaching out, to being there for Mary in whatever ways she could.

Hannah's thoughts remained on Mary as she tidied up the kitchen, putting away the last of the baking supplies. The bell above the door gave a jingle, announcing a customer.

"I'll be with you in just a sec," Hannah called, dusting off her apron.

She stepped out of the kitchen to find Daniel standing behind the counter, hat in hand and a hesitant smile on his face.

"*Gude daag*, Hannah."

"Daniel," Hannah replied with a polite smile. "What brings you here?"

Daniel shifted from one foot to the other, evidently uncomfortable. "I came to buy some pastries."

Hannah gestured to the display case filled with an assortment of delicious baked goods. "Well, you've *kumm* to the right place. What can I get for you?"

Daniel's gaze scanned the pastries, but he didn't seem to be focusing on them.

Finally, he took a deep breath and looked at her directly. "I've been wanting to talk to you about something."

After an expectant pause, Daniel finally continued. "Hannah, I've spoken to your *vadder...*"

Hannah's heart skipped a beat and gave an uneasy thud. "*Ach?*"

Daniel took a deep breath, his gaze holding hers. "I want us to start courting officially. Your *vadder* thinks it's a *gut* idea."

Hannah felt a brief sense of losing her balance, of dizziness. She gripped the counter to balance herself. "Daniel, I..."

But before she could gather her thoughts, the bell above the door announced more customers. Levi and his sister, Rachel, walked in, their presence an unexpected but welcome interruption. Daniel's face pulled into a frown, but Hannah quickly composed herself and received them warmly.

"Levi, Rachel! It's *gut* to see you both," Hannah greeted, her smile genuine.

"*Gude daag*, Hannah," Rachel returned.

Hannah met Levi's eyes, and he smiled warmly at her; however, she could not ignore Daniel, who also had his eyes firmly fixed on her, practically boring into her. She quickly redirected her gaze.

"What can I get for you?" she asked Rachel.

"I was hoping to get some of your shoofly

pies."

Hannah nodded. "Of course," she replied. "I've just finished a batch this morning. Let me get some for you."

She carefully selected a few pieces of shoofly pie, placing them into a box. The rich scent of molasses and spices filled the air, mingling deliciously with the other scents lingering in the bakery.

"I must say *danki*," Rachel said as Hannah worked.

"For what?" Hannah asked, not looking up from her task.

"For helping my *bruder* get a job with Mr. Fisher."

"*Ach*," Hannah deflected. "I didn't really do anything."

"I didn't know you were working with Isaac," Daniel directed at Levi, his tone rather sharp.

Levi shrugged, trying to keep the atmosphere light. "*Ya*," he said simply.

The bakery fell silent, and Hannah could sense the tension between the two men.

"Well, I should be going," Daniel finally said. "*Danki* for the pastries, Hannah." He gave a curt nod to Levi and Rachel before turning to leave.

"*Sei gut*, Daniel," Hannah called, her voice gentle.

As the door closed behind him, Levi turned to Hannah, a hint of concern in his eyes. "Did I interrupt something?"

Hannah shook her head, waving off his concern. "*Nee*, it's all right. Daniel...he came to buy pastries."

Rachel raised an eyebrow, sensing there was more to the story but wisely not pressing.

"Here you go," Hannah said, handing Rachel the box.

"*Danki*," said Rachel as she accepted the box with a grateful smile.

Again, the room fell silent. Rachel glanced between Hannah and Levi.

"Well I should get home," she said. "*Bis widder*, Hannah."

Hannah smiled as Rachel turned to go, leaving them alone. The air felt charged, a subtle but undeniable tensity hanging between them. She busied herself with tidying up the counter, her mind racing with thoughts she couldn't quite articulate. She could sense Levi's probing gaze.

"So, how are things going with Isaac?" she

asked, glancing up at Levi.

Levi leaned against the counter, his expression thoughtful. "Really well, actually."

Hannah smiled, pleased to hear the positive report.

After a brief pause, Levi cleared his throat, breaking the tension. "Are you going to the school *Grischtdaag* program tomorrow?"

Hannah nodded, her heart beating a little faster. "*Ya*, I am. I'm helping with the decorations. What about you?"

"I'll be there," Levi confirmed. "Rachel roped me into helping with some of the setup."

The room fell silent again, but the energy between the two was palpable.

"I should probably get back to work," Levi said somewhat reluctantly.

Hannah nodded as Levi turned to go.

"Wait!" Hannah suddenly called out.

He turned back to her, his expression one of hope.

"Let me give you some pastries for Isaac," said Hannah.

Levi nodded, watching as Hannah deftly boxed up some fresh pastries. As she handed him the box, their fingers brushed, and her heart skittered in her chest. The contact sent a jolt through her, and she almost dropped the box.

"*Ach*, sorry!" she exclaimed, flustered. "Butterfingers are a hazard of the job."

Levi chuckled, his eyes sparkling with amusement. "*Nee* problem at all."

Hannah felt her cheeks flush and laughed softly, her embarrassment mingling with a growing warmth. "I'll see you at the school tomorrow."

Levi nodded, his grin widening. "See you tomorrow."

Their eyes lingered momentarily on each other. Levi's smile warmed Hannah from head to toe, filling her with a sense of anticipation she hadn't felt in a long time. As he turned to leave, the bell above the door chimed softly, and Hannah watched him go, her heart still aflutter.

That evening, after closing up the bakery, Hannah walked home through the quiet streets of Willowvale. The sky was darkening and the stars just beginning to twinkle in the crisp dusk air. Her thoughts were a jumble, drifting from the electricity she had felt when with Levi to the looming conversation she knew she would be forced to have with her father.

Hannah entered the house quietly, the familiar scents of home enveloping her and calming her slightly. She hung her coat on the peg by the door and slipped off her shoes, feeling the smooth wooden floor under her feet. The sound of her father's voice, soft and rhythmic, reached her ears. She made her way to the study.

Her father, Bishop Weaver, was seated at his desk, surrounded by books and papers. The flickering light from the kerosene lamp cast a soft glow over his thoughtful face as he worked on his sermon. He looked up briefly, his eyes softening when he saw her.

"*Guder owed*, Hannah," he said with a gentle smile.

"*Guder owed*, *Vadder*," she replied, popping her head into the room. "How's the sermon coming along?"

"It's coming together," he affirmed, setting his pen down. "Just trying to find the right words. How was your day at the bakery?"

Hannah stepped into the room, leaning

against the doorframe. "It was *gut*. Mary came by to help for a bit."

Her father nodded, his eyes reflecting both interest and understanding. "That's *gut* to hear. It's important for Mary to feel connected to the *gmay*."

Hannah nodded, her thoughts briefly drifting back to the bakery and her interaction with Levi. "*Ya*, it is. I'm glad she came."

Bishop Weaver nodded.

"I'll get started on dinner," said Hannah.

She left the study and made her way to the kitchen—a cozy room, with its wooden cabinets and the faint scent of spices in the air—where she lit the stove and set a pot of water to boil, pulling out ingredients for a simple but hearty meal.

As Hannah chopped vegetables and prepared the dough for bread, her mind wandered back to the day's encounter with Levi. She could still feel the warmth of his touch and the way his smile had made her heart flutter and her belly do a backflip. She shook her head slightly, trying to focus on the task at hand.

Soon, the aroma of mixed vegetable stew filled the kitchen. Hannah hummed a hymn as she worked, the melody both peaceful and comforting. She set the table, laying out simple but tasteful pottery plates, and placed the bread in the oven.

As she stirred the stew, Hannah contemplated about the upcoming school Christmas program and how much she was looking forward to seeing Levi again. The thought brought a small smile to her lips, and she silently prayed for guidance and clarity, asking God to give her wisdom in whether or not to pursue more than a friendship with Levi and trusting Him that whatever was meant to be would become clear in time.

The sound of her father's footsteps on the stairs pulled her from her reflection. He entered the kitchen, the lines of concentration on his face softening at the sight of dinner being prepared.

"Something smells *gut*," he said, sitting down at the table.

Hannah smiled, placing the pot of stew on the tabletop before taking a seat across from her father.

They bowed their heads in a silent prayer of thanks before dishing up their meal. After a brief silence as they ate, Hannah's father set his fork down and cleared his throat. Hannah looked across at him, swallowing past her heart, which was in her throat.

"I had a visitor today," he began, his voice steady and authoritative. "Daniel King came to see me."

Hannah nodded as she took a tiny bite of bread. She knew what was coming next.

"Daniel is a nice young *mann* from a *gut*, traditional *familye*. He spoke to me about wanting to court you officially."

Hannah forced herself to meet her father's gaze, her mind racing like a cornered jackrabbit. "*Vadder*, I know Daniel is a *gut mann*. But…".

Bishop Weaver raised an eyebrow, his expression serious. "But what, Hannah?"

She took a deep breath, trying to find the right words. "Daniel is my friend, and I know he would make a fine *mann*. But…I want more than just a *gut* match. I want love."

Her father's stoic expression softened slightly, but his eyes remained steadfast. "Love is important, Hannah, but so is practicality. You're in your mid-twenties now, and many of your friends are already married with *kinner*. It's time to consider your future seriously."

Hannah rested her cutlery on the rim of her plate and looked down at her hands, her heart aching. "I know, *Vadder*. But I can't give up on finding the right person for me, someone whom I feel like I can't live without, not just someone I feel I can live with and build a life with."

Her father sighed, his stern demeanor giving way to concern. "Hannah, I want what's best for you. Daniel is a *gut* match. He cares for you and has a stable future. Sometimes, love grows over time. It's not always immediate."

Hannah nodded, her eyes glistening with unshed tears. "I understand, *Vadder*," she said. "I will think and pray about it."

The remainder of the meal passed in a more subdued silence. Hannah's thoughts circled back to Levi and the way he made her feel earlier that day in the bakery. It was different from anything she had ever experienced with Daniel—more electric, more authentic.

After dinner, Hannah washed the dishes, the familiar routine offering some comfort, while her father retired to his study, leaving her alone with her thoughts.

Later, as she sat by the window in her room,

looking out at the stars, she couldn't help but feel a sense of longing. She wanted what her parents had—a marriage built on mutual respect and genuine love. She worried that settling for less might lead to regret.

As she lay in bed, the house quiet around her, Hannah prayed for guidance. She asked for the strength to follow her heart, too, even if it meant going against the expectations of her community and her family.

Chapter Six

Levi walked down the path toward the schoolhouse. Anna and Eli raced ahead while Rachel and Conrad walked hand in hand beside Levi. This was his first Amish community gathering in Willowvale, and as much as he wanted to enjoy it, an ache gnawed in the pit of his stomach. He'd always loved Christmas, but now, things were painfully different.

As they approached the schoolhouse, with evergreen garlands adorning the windows and doorways, Levi paused.

Rachel placed a gentle hand on his arm. "Levi, are you all right?" she asked softly, her eyes filled with concern.

Levi took a deep breath, forcing a smile. "I'm

fine."

Rachel's expression softened, her eyes reflecting the shared pain and understanding between them. "It's hard, I know," she said quietly. "But we have each other."

Levi nodded, his throat tight with emotion. "I know. It's just...everything feels different this year."

Rachel squeezed his arm reassuringly. "It does, but that's okay. We can still make new memories and honor the old ones. *Maem* and *Daed* would want us to find joy even in the midst of our grief."

Levi did his best to give a sincere smile.

"*Kumm* on, let's go inside," said Rachel.

With a deep breath, Levi nodded and allowed Rachel to lead him into the schoolhouse. The entrance was flanked by two small fir trees, each decorated with handmade ornaments crafted by the children. Inside, handmade paper snowflakes hung from the ceiling, and the sound of cheerful chatter and laughter filled the room.

The long wooden benches were arranged to face a small stage at the front of the room, where a colorful backdrop painted with a winter scene provided the perfect setting for the

Christmas performances. Candles placed along the windowsills flickered softly, casting a soft glow over the room.

Levi took a deep breath, feeling a little overwhelmed by the bustling crowd. Families were gathered in small groups, talking and laughing, while students ran around, their faces bright with excitement. The room was filled with the smell of freshly baked cookies and the crisp scent of pine.

As he scanned the room, his eyes came to rest on Hannah. She was helping some of the children get ready, and her cheerful presence was immediately calming. When she looked up and saw him, her face cracked into a wide smile. She excused herself and walked over to him, her eyes sparkling with the joy of the season.

"Levi, you made it!" she said, her voice filled with genuine pleasure.

Levi felt the knots in his stomach unravel at the sight of her. "I did. It looks *wunderbaar*."

Hannah beamed. "The *kinner* worked so hard on the decorations."

Levi looked around, taking in the festive atmosphere. "It's really impressive. You can feel the *Grischtdaag* spirit everywhere."

Hannah nodded, her eyes wistful. "It's one of my favorite times of the year. The *gmay* comes together, and you can see the joy it brings to everyone."

Levi felt a wave of gratitude for Hannah's presence; she had a way of making him feel welcome and at ease.

"*Kumm* on, let me introduce you to some people."

She led him through the room, introducing him to various members of the community. Levi met farmers, shop owners, and housewives, each greeting him with warmth and friendliness. The only person who didn't appear pleased to see him was Daniel King, who glared at him from across the room. Levi, however, did his best to ignore him.

As they moved through the crowd, Levi's apprehension dissipated and was replaced by a growing sense of belonging. The nervousness that had gripped him earlier faded, and a warm feeling of acceptance pervaded his heart. Hannah stayed by his side, her presence a constant source of comfort.

Just then, the schoolmistress, Miss Miller, called for everyone to take their seats. Levi found a seat near the front with Rachel and Conrad, while Hannah took a seat beside her father in the front row.

"*Guder owed*, everyone, and *willkumm* to our annual *Grischtdaag* program," Miss Miller began as she gazed around the room. "We are so pleased to see so many of you gathered together here tonight to celebrate this joyous season. This evening is a special time for us to *kumm* together as a *gmay* and to reflect on the true meaning of *Grischtdaag*."

A poignant pause.

"Our *kinner* have worked very hard to prepare this program for you. They have put their hearts into every poem and song, and I am sure you will be as proud of them as I am. Tonight, we will hear traditional carols and listen to the heartfelt little verses the *kinner* will recite as they bring the story of *Grischtdaag* to life."

She turned to smile at the students, who smiled back at her.

"But beyond the performances, this evening is about coming together to share in the spirit of love, generosity, and gratitude that this season brings. It is a time to remember the simple pleasures of life and the deep meaning of *Grischtdaag*, to celebrate the birth of Jesus, and to nurture the bonds that hold our *gmay* together. So without further ado, let us begin our program. I invite you all to sit back, relax, and let the warmth of this special evening fill your hearts. *Danki*, and *Frehlicher Grischtdaag*."

Applause erupted as the children stepped forward.

The program began with the singing of traditional Christmas carols. The older students came to the front of the room, their hands folded neatly in front of them as they began to sing.

> *"Stille Nacht, heilige Nacht,*
> *Alles schläft, einsam wacht*
> *Nur das traute, hochheilige Paar.*
> *Holder Knabe im lockigen Haar,*
> *Schlaf in himmlischer Ruh,*
> *Schlaf in himmlischer Ruh."*

A wave of nostalgic warmth washed over Levi as he listened to the familiar song, the words bringing back pleasant memories of past Christmases.

Next, came the younger children, which included Anna and Eli. Their voices were high and clear in song.

> *"Ihr Kinderlein, kommet, o kommet doch all,*
> *Zur Krippe her kommet in Bethlehems Stall*
> *Und seht, was in dieser hochheiligen Nacht*
> *Der Vater im Himmel für Freude uns macht."*

After the carols, the older children came forward and began to recite "The Christmas Story."

> *In Bethlehem, that wondrous night,*
> *A star shone down, so pure, so bright.*
> *The shepherds watched their flocks with care,*
> *When angels sang in the cold night air.*

> *"Fear not," they said, "for we bring news*
> *Of great joy that's meant for you.*
> *In a manger, meek and mild,*
> *Lies the Christ, the holy Child."*

> *The shepherds hurried to the place,*
> *Where they found the baby's face.*
> *Wrapped in cloth, in a manger bed,*
> *The promised Savior lay His head.*

> *Three wise men traveled from afar,*
> *Guided by that shining star.*
> *With gifts of gold and frankincense,*

And myrrh, they brought their reverence.

They knelt before the Holy One,
God's own perfect, precious Son.
Born to bring us peace and light,
On that blessed, silent night.

The stable's humble setting shone,
As Heaven's love made earth its home.
For unto us a child is given,
The greatest gift from God in Heaven.

So let us sing and let us praise,
With thankful hearts our voices raise.
For in that stable, dark and cold,
The greatest story ever told.

The room exploded once more into applause, the atmosphere vibrant and alive with the spirit of the true reason for the season—celebrating Jesus. Levi glanced at Hannah, who was watching the performances with an expression of pride and affection. A surge of admiration for her, not just for her beauty but for her kindness and the way she cared for those around her, surged through him.

The last item on the Christmas program was a poem recited by the younger children, who looked both excited and nervous as they began.

A simple gift, wrapped up with care,
Is given with love, a treasure rare.
For in this season, hearts are full,
And blessings shared make spirits whole.

A handmade scarf, so soft and warm,
A token of love to weather the storm.
A pie baked fresh, its crust so sweet,
A neighborly gift, a heartfelt treat.

A child's small drawing, colors bright,
A message of joy in every line and light.
A hug, a smile, a listening ear,
Small acts of kindness that bring us near.

In giving, we find the truest cheer,
For love and joy grow year by year.
A simple gift, no matter how small,
Can be the greatest gift of all.

So in this season, let us find
The joy in giving, hearts entwined.
For gifts of love, both great and slight,
Bring warmth and light on a winter's night.

As the final words of the poem faded, the audience stood and gave a standing ovation. The children's faces shone with pride and joy as their hard work was rewarded by the warm reception. Miss Miller returned to the stage, beaming with satisfaction. She raised her hands to still the crowd.

"*Danki*, everyone, for being such a *wunderbaar* audience," she gushed, her voice filled with pride. "Our *kinner* have truly brought the spirit of *Grischtdaag* alive tonight with their beautiful performances. Let us give them one more round of applause."

Applause echoed through the schoolhouse once again. Miss Miller waited for the sound to die down before continuing.

"Now, we invite you all to stay and enjoy some refreshments provided by Mrs. Bontrager and Hannah Weaver from the bakery. There are plenty of *appetditlich* treats and warm drinks to share, so please, make yourselves comfortable and enjoy the rest of the evening with friends and *familye*."

Miss Miller stepped down from the stage, and the crowd began to stir. Parents moved forward to congratulate their children, and the room buzzed with conversation and laughter.

"*Onkel* Levi!" Anna called as she and her

brother hurried towards them. "Did you like it?"

"Like it? I loved it! You were both *wunderbaar*," praised Levi.

Anna flushed with pride.

"I thought I was going to forget my words, but I didn't!" Eli said, beaming.

Levi chuckled, ruffling Eli's hair. "You were fantastic, Eli. You both were. You should be very proud of yourselves."

Anna and Eli chattered on animatedly as Levi's gaze moved over the crowd, seeking out Hannah. He finally spotted her near the refreshment table, talking to a group of parents.

"I'll be right back," said Levi.

He weaved his way through the throng of people, his heart beating a little faster as he approached Hannah. Just then, though, he spotted Isaac standing alone near the window. Shortly after he started working for Isaac, Rachel shared with Levi what the Fishers had gone through, losing their only child to illness. He had not spoken to Isaac about it because he understood all too well the deep, aching void that grief left behind. But seeing Isaac standing there all alone, his sorrow evident in the stoop of his posture, Levi felt compelled to reach out.

"Isaac," Levi greeted warmly as he walked over to him. "I didn't know you were coming tonight."

Isaac looked up at him, uncertainty etched into his expression. "I wasn't sure I was coming," he murmured. "But I thought maybe…"

His shoulders sagged, and his voice trailed off as he looked out the window again in wistfulness.

Levi nodded. "The *kinner* did a fantastic job."

"They did," Isaac agreed.

"Mary not with you tonight?" Levi enquired, glancing around automatically trying to catch a glimpse of her.

"*Nee,*" Isaac sighed. "She's…she's having a tough time. And tonight, well, Grace was part of the program last year, and she…she just thought it would be too hard."

Levi didn't answer for a moment, wishing he knew the right words to utter.

"Isaac—"

"Well I should get back to Mary," Isaac interrupted. "I'll see you tomorrow."

Without another word, Isaac turned to go, leaving Levi alone. Levi watched him. He had walked in the man's shoes and knew what

Isaac was feeling and experiencing—wave after wave of grief that hit a person relentlessly one after another and pulled them under, leaving them desperate for air, only to whip them back under just when they surfaced, lungs aflame, bursting for life-giving air. Christmas had always been a time of happiness and togetherness for Levi's family. That year, however, everything was different. The loss of his parents cast a shadow over the holiday. Every song, every decoration, every small insignificant thing reminded him of happier times—that were now gone. Pain stabbed Levi's heart; he missed his parents more than ever.

His morose thoughts were abruptly interrupted by the sound of raised voices. Levi turned to see Hannah and Daniel in the corner of the schoolhouse, their faces tense with emotion, mid-argument. He couldn't hear all the words, but it was very clear that the discussion was heated.

Daniel's face was flushed, while Hannah wore an expression of frustration and determination. Instinctively, Levi made his way over to them. Daniel noticed his approach and fell silent, his mouth pulling into a grim line and his expression hardening.

"Levi," he said curtly, acknowledging his presence but clearly not pleased by the interruption.

Hannah turned, her eyes softening when she saw Levi.

"I just wanted to make sure everything's okay," Levi stated, his gaze bouncing between the two.

Daniel's eyes flashed with irritation. "Everything's fine," he said sharply.

Hannah stepped closer to Levi, her hand lightly touching his arm. "Daniel," she said, directing her gaze back to Daniel. "I think it's best if we continue this conversation later."

Daniel looked between them, his jaw clenched, but he nodded reluctantly. "Fine. We'll talk later."

He turned and stalked off, leaving Hannah and Levi standing together.

Levi dipped his gaze to meet Hannah's, concern crinkling his features. "Are you all right?"

Hannah sighed, her shoulders relaxing slightly. "I'm fine," she said, doing her best to smile, but it faltered. "Actually, I think I am ready to go home."

"I'll walk with you," Levi offered.

They slipped out of the schoolhouse into the cool night, the crisp air a welcome change from the warm, bustling interior.

They walked in silence for a while under the brightly twinkling stars overhead, and every now and then, Levi glanced at Hannah, noting her distant expression.

"Isaac came to the school tonight," Levi said, breaking the silence.

Hannah nodded, her countenance somber. "It's been incredibly hard for both Isaac and Mary since Grace passed. I was hoping Mary might *kumm* tonight."

"I can't begin to imagine what they are going through," Levi said sadly.

Hannah exhaled softly. "Mary and Levi tried for years to have *kinner*. They had almost given up when Grace came along. She was their miracle *kind*."

Levi's heart ached for them.

"I've been trying to help Mary," continued Hannah. "But it's a long road to healing."

They fell silent again, the night's quietude enveloping them. Soon, they turned into the snowy street, passing by the warmly lit houses.

"Well, this is me," said Hannah as they reached the house at the end of the street.

Levi turned to her.

"Levi," Hannah ventured. "When I asked you why you came to Willowvale, you said you wanted a fresh start."

"That's right," Levi confirmed.

"May I ask what happened to warrant you feeling like that?"

Levi hesitated as he held Hannah's gaze. He'd never talked about what happened, usually sidestepping the issue because it was too painful, but something in her expression evoked trust in him that she would understand.

"My *eldre* died in an accident earlier this year. It was sudden and…it left a huge void in my life."

"*Ach*, Levi," Hannah said, her eyes misting in compassion. "I am so sorry."

Levi exhaled shakily. "Rachel was already living here, and she kept telling me about this place. I thought maybe a fresh start would help me heal, move on…"

His voice trailed off, and to his surprise, Hannah reached out and gently brushed his arm with her fingertips. The warmth of her touch sent a jolt through him, and his heart skipped a beat as he lost himself in her eyes. The world around them briefly stood still as his breath caught in his throat.

A throat clearing loudly behind them brought the present sharply back into focus. They turned in unison to see Bishop Weaver standing on the porch, watching them.

"*Vadder*," Hannah said, her voice rising slightly in her nervousness. "This is Levi Miller."

Levi stepped forward. "It's a pleasure to meet you, Bishop Weaver."

The Bishop nodded, his expression not particularly warm. "It's late," was all he said.

Hannah glanced at Levi apologetically. "I should go inside. *Danki* for walking with me, Levi. I'll see you tomorrow."

Levi smiled. "*Gude nacht*, Hannah."

Levi took his time walking back to Rachel's house, mulling over the evening's events. The cool night air couldn't diminish the warmth he felt from being with Hannah. The gentle touch of her fingers on his arm lingered, sending ripples of unfamiliar yet welcome emotions coursing through him.

Levi's thoughts drifted back to Emma—the

woman he had been planning to marry before his parents' accident changed everything. Emma had been a good match—kind, thoughtful, and well-suited to the life they envisioned together. But the feelings he had for her, though genuine, had never sparked the same intense emotion he experienced when he was around Hannah.

With Emma, everything was predictable and comfortable. They had known each other for years, their families approving of the union. Yet, something was always missing, a spark he hadn't quite been able to identify. When the tragedy struck, it was as if the fragile thread that held them together snapped, and their relationship dissolved in the wake of his grief.

Levi shook his head, trying to grasp the strange, exciting, and somewhat terrifying feelings that were now rising up within him. He had never expected to feel this way, especially not so soon after losing his parents and ending his engagement. The intensity of his emotions for Hannah was simultaneously exhilarating and daunting.

He thought about the way her eyes lit up when she smiled, the kindness and strength she exuded in every action, and the way she listened to him, genuinely caring about his feelings. There was something deeply compelling about her, something that drew him in and made him feel alive in a way he hadn't felt in a long time.

As he walked under the starlit sky, Levi wondered if he was truly ready to open his heart again after so much loss. It felt risky, but the connection he felt with Hannah was undeniable. It was a strange feeling, knowing that something new and potentially beautiful was sprouting out of the remnants of his old life, like green shoots emerging after a fire razes a pasture.

The familiar warmth of home greeted him as he reached Rachel's house. He paused at the door, taking a deep breath. Despite the uncertainty and the fear of being hurt again, Levi knew he didn't want to turn away from this new path. The future, with all its unknowns, suddenly seemed a little brighter and filled with possibility.

Chapter Seven

Mary sat alone in Grace's room. The small kerosene lamp cast a dull gloomy light within its walls as she stared out of the window at the softly falling snow. She couldn't bear even the thought of going to the school and seeing all the families with their children—their laughter and joy would amplify her own intense sense of loss. So, instead, she had stayed home, seeking solace in the room that still felt so intimately connected to Grace.

Mary's thoughts drifted back to the previous year's Christmas program. Grace had been so excited, her eyes shining with anticipation as she diligently practiced her songs and lines over and over again. Mary remembered helping her into a little red dress, the one with the white lace collar, and braiding her hair with festive ribbons.

Grace had stood on that stage, her voice clear and sweet as she sang "Silent Night" with the other children. Mary had watched from the audience, her heart swollen with pride and joy. Isaac had been beside her, his arm draped affectionately around her shoulders, both of them filled with the wonder of the season and the simple contentment of seeing Grace so full of life and joy.

Tears welled up in Mary's eyes as she thought about how different everything now was. Her grief felt unbearable at times, almost as though all four walls of a room were closing in on her and she couldn't escape. She missed Grace with an intensity that sometimes felt suffocating, the pain sharp and unrelenting.

The double click of the front door opening and closing pulled Mary from her reverie. A few moments later, Isaac appeared in the doorway, his presence barely registering in Mary's consciousness. She looked up at him, her eyes tired and hollow.

"I wish you'd gone with me tonight," Isaac said softly.

Mary shook her head, her voice barely above a whisper. "I couldn't face it, Isaac. Not tonight."

Isaac nodded, weariness and sorrow etched on his face. Isaac wordlessly walked into the room and sat beside Mary on the bed. Mary turned away from him, her body tense and unyielding. She felt him reach out, his hand trying to take hers, but she leaned away, wrapping her arms tightly around herself.

"Mary," he said, his voice laced with pain and frustration.

But her stony silence and stiff body language formed a barrier between them. Isaac sat there for a moment, his hand hovering in the air before he let it drop. He sighed heavily, a sound filled with helplessness.

After a pause, he got up and moved toward the doorway. He hesitated, his back to her, his shoulders slumped. "We can't go on like this, Mary. I lost a *dochder*, too, and now I have to stand by and watch my *fraa* disappear right in front of me? I can't do it. I can't just stand back and watch you slip away."

Mary's heart ached at his frank declaration, but she remained silent, unable to give him comfort or reassurance. When she finally turned to look at him, Isaac was gone, his footsteps echoing faintly down the hallway.

She sat motionless, the quiet of the house closing in around her, making breathing difficult. The sound of Isaac in his workshop reached her ears. As she considered the state of their marriage, guilt and sorrow weighed heavily on her heart.

Their early years of marriage were filled with so much love and laughter. They had been young and full of dreams, building their life together in their cozy home. She remembered the long evenings spent talking about their hopes for the future. Isaac's warm laughter had echoed through the house as they found a simple joy from being in each other's company.

Yet, amidst the happiness were hardships, too. They had dreamed of filling their home with the laughter of their sons and daughters, but as the years passed, it became clear that their dreams of a large family would never come to fruition. Mary remembered all too well the countless nights she had cried herself to sleep from the pain of each passing month without a sign of pregnancy. She thought back on the visits to the doctor, the endless prayers, the countless times of hope dashed by disappointment; Proverbs 13:12—"Hope deferred makes the heart sick"—had been her experience many a month.

But Isaac was her rock through it all. He had held her when she cried, whispered words of comfort and encouragement, and never once let her face their struggles alone. They had come to terms with the possibility of never having children, finding solace and strength in their love for each other and in their ultimate Rock, God. Isaac's unwavering faith and gentle support had kept her going even when she felt like giving up.

Then, when they had least expected it, God gave them a miracle. Mary discovered she was pregnant, and their joy knew no bounds. The months of waiting, praying, and hoping had culminated in the birth of their beautiful daughter, Grace. She was their miracle child, the answer to their prayers and the sun in their lives. The joy of her arrival brought them even closer, with their love for each other deepening as they marveled at the precious gift they had been given.

Those days were filled with happiness and contentment, watching Grace grow and flourish, her laughter filling their home with warmth. Isaac had been a devoted father, his eyes lighting up whenever he looked at Grace. They shared so many precious moments, each one a testament to their lasting love and the family they had finally become.

But now, all that had been lost. The joy that Grace had brought into their lives was gone, replaced by a deep, interminable and insurmountable grief that seemed impossible to overcome. The house that had once been filled with laughter now felt hollow, empty, and cold. The pain of losing Grace had collapsed her world, and Mary was drowning in her sorrow, unable to find her way back to the life they once knew.

Mary closed her eyes and squeezed them tightly in agony, the tears finally spilling over. She wanted to reach out to Isaac, to tell him she was sorry, to let him hold her and share in their pain. But she was trapped in the labyrinth of her grief.

That night, Mary lay in the darkness as the

silence of the house pressed down on her. The space beside her was empty, the sheets cold and stiff. Like so many other nights, Isaac wouldn't be coming to bed.

She stared at the ceiling, willing the sweet oblivion of sleep to come. It was her only escape, but the emptiness in the bed beside her was a cold reminder that the joy had been snatched from their lives. She turned on her side, clutching Grace's quilt to her chest, seeking solace in its familiar feel and scent.

Mary lay there for hours, her mind a whirlwind of memories and pain. Finally, exhaustion took over and she drifted into a restless sleep. In her dreams, she was at the park with Grace. The sun was shining and the air filled with children's laughter. Grace's bright smile lit up her entire face as she ran through the grass, her laughter echoing in the warm breeze. Mary watched her daughter, her heart full and the pain and sorrow of reality forgotten.

But suddenly, the dream shifted. The park grew darker, the laughter faded. Mary looked around, panic rising in her chest. Grace was gone. She called out to her, her voice trembling with fear.

"Grace! Grace, where are you?"

She ran through the park, searching frantically, but there was no sign of her daughter. The trees seemed to close in around her, the darkness growing thicker. Desperation clawed at her heart as she called out again.

"Grace! Please, come back!"

Mary woke with a start, her heart pounding in her chest. The panic from her dream clung to her, her skin having broken out into a cold sweat. She sat up, gasping for breath, the image of the empty park and her missing daughter dancing before her.

"I need to find Grace," she whispered to herself, her voice shaky and desperate.

She threw back the covers and climbed out of bed, not bothering to change out of her nightgown. Driven by an overwhelming need to find her daughter, Mary hurried through the house and out the front door, the icy night air biting through her skin. She didn't care. She had to get to the park.

The park was dark and silent, and the moonlight cast eerie shadows on the playground equipment. Mary's breath came in short ragged gasps as she ran to the spot where she had last seen Grace in her dream. She called out her daughter's name, her voice juddering with desperation.

"Grace! Grace, where are you?"

Tears streamed down Mary's face as she looked around, the panic from her dream now a living, breathing nightmare.

"Grace, please! Come back to me!"

The only sound was the rustling of leaves in the wind. Mary fell to her knees, her body shaking with sobs. She was alone, more alone than she had ever felt in her life.

"Please, *Gott*," she whispered, her voice breaking. "Help me find my way back to her. Help me find my way back to myself."

As she knelt there in the darkness, the reality of her loss washed over Mary afresh. Grace was gone, and no amount of searching would bring her back. Mary's body ached, and the chill of the night seeped into her bones, but she knew she had to keep moving forward.

Slowly, Mary got to her feet. However, in the darkness, she stumbled over a patch of uneven ground, her hands and knees scraping against the rough earth. Her head hit the ground, and the world went in and out of focus before everything turned dark.

Chapter Eight

I saac woke early the next morning as the faint light of dawn filtering through the small window of his workshop lightly feathered his face. He had spent another restless night on the narrow cot, his mind in turmoil with thoughts of Mary and the growing distance between them. With a sigh, he swung his legs off the cot side, got up, and stretched, his muscles protesting the uncomfortable sleeping arrangement.

He slowly made his way to the house. When he stepped inside, the house was quiet. Too quiet. The kind of silence that made his heart pound with unease.

"Mary?" he called out, his voice reverberating hollowly in the empty hallway.

He went to their bedroom first, pushing the door open with a sense of trepidation. The bed was unmade, and the covers were thrown back as if Mary had left in a hurry. The room felt cold and unwelcoming, a stark contrast to the warmth it had once held.

Isaac moved through the house, checking each room as he went. The kitchen was empty, the hearth cold. The living room, with the quilt Mary had been working on draped over the arm of the chair, was similarly devoid of life. Apprehension gave way to panic as the fear that something might have happened to Mary gripped his heart.

He paused in the kitchen, trying to think clearly. Mary wouldn't have just left without saying something. She must have gone somewhere familiar, somewhere she felt safe. The bakery. Of course. She must have gone to see Hannah. The thought brought Isaac a measure of relief, and he quickly grabbed his coat and made his way out the door.

As he walked through the village, the early morning light cast long shadows on the snow-caked ground. The familiar path to the bakery brought back memories of happier times when he and Mary had walked hand in hand, dreaming of their future. Now, those dreams felt shattered, replaced by a reality neither of them knew how to navigate.

The warm light from the bakery windows was a welcome sight. Isaac stepped inside to the rich scent of freshly baked bread and pastries. Hannah, who was behind the counter arranging a tray of cookies, looked up as the bell above the door chimed, her face lighting up with a smile that dissolved into concern when she saw him.

"Isaac," she greeted, wiping her hands on her apron. "What brings you by so early?"

Isaac scanned the room, but there was no sign of Mary. "I was hoping Mary was here. I woke up this morning, and she was gone. I thought she might have *kumm* to see you."

Hannah's smile faltered slightly with concern flickering in her eyes. "*Nee*, I haven't seen her yet. Do you think something is amiss?"

Isaac sighed, running a hand through his hair. "I don't know. I woke up, and she was gone. The bed was unmade, and she didn't leave a note or anything."

Hannah set the tray down and came around the counter, her expression serious.

"I can help you look for her. Maybe someone in town has seen her."

Isaac nodded.

Hannah grabbed her shawl. "Let's start with Main Street. She might have just gone for a walk."

They stepped out into the crisp morning air as the sun climbed higher in the sky. The village was starting to come to life with people going about their morning routines. Isaac and Hannah made their way down Main Street, stopping to ask anyone they saw if they had seen Mary.

"Excuse me, have you seen Mary this morning?" Isaac asked Mr. Yoder, who was opening up his general store.

Mr. Yoder shook his head, a frown creasing his brow. "*Nee*, I haven't seen her, Isaac. Is everything all right?"

"We're not sure," Hannah interjected. "We're just trying to find her."

They continued down the street, asking neighbors and shopkeepers, but no one had seen Mary. With each passing minute, Isaac's worry multiplied. He tried to stay calm, but the fear of losing her, too, was overwhelming. He mentally took a moment to ask the One who knew where she was to please look after her and help him find his beloved Mary.

They reached the edge of the village, having exhausted all other possibilities.

"What about the park?" Hannah suggested.

Isaac's eyes widened with realization. "Of course! The park. Let's go."

They hurried toward the park, their footsteps quickening as the urgency of their search intensified.

Just then, they bumped into Levi.

"Isaac, Hannah," Levi greeted with a smile that quickly faded as he noticed their anxious expressions. "I was just on my way to the workshop. What's going on? Is everything all right?"

Isaac shook his head, his voice tight as he answered, "It's Mary. She's missing. I woke up this morning, and she was gone. We've been searching the village, but no one has seen her."

Levi's face hardened with determination. "I'll help you look for her. Where have you checked so far?"

"We've asked around town and were heading to the park," Hannah explained.

Levi nodded. "I'll go with you."

Isaac's heart thudded in his chest, each step

bringing him closer to finding Mary—or so he hoped. The park, a small peaceful area with trees and benches scattered throughout, finally came into view.

He scanned the park as his heart pounded with fear. His eyes suddenly caught sight of a motionless figure lying on the ground, covered in a thin layer of snow. His heart momentarily stopped, and his stomach sank.

"Mary!" he called, his voice choked with panic as he rushed over to her.

He dropped to his knees beside her, gently rolling her over. Her skin was icy, her body stiff.

"Mary?" Can you hear me?" he urged, his voice trembling.

He leaned in close and pressed his ear against her chest to check for signs of life. He listened desperately and then heard it—a faint irregular heartbeat. A whimper of relief escaped his lips.

"We need to get her home and warmed up," Hannah pressed, her face pale with alarm. She turned to Levi. "Fetch the doctor. Quickly!"

Levi nodded and took off at a sprint, not wasting a moment. Isaac gathered Mary into his arms, her cold limp body feeling too light and fragile. He cradled her close, trying to share his body heat as he carried her back towards their house.

The journey home felt like an eternity, each step heavy with concern. Isaac whispered words of encouragement to Mary, his breath clouding in the frigid air. "Hold on, Mary. Please, just hold on."

Hannah walked beside them with her hand on Isaac's arm, offering silent support. As they reached the house, Isaac pushed the door open with his shoulder and carried Mary inside.

He laid her gently on the couch before grabbing blankets and wrapping them snugly around her. Hannah stoked the fire, adding more wood to increase the heat. They worked quickly, their movements synchronized by a shared sense of urgency and fear.

"She's so cold," Isaac murmured, his hands shaking as he rubbed her arms and legs, trying to stimulate circulation. "Mary, stay with me. Please."

Hannah brought hot water bottles, placing them around Mary's body to help warm her. "We need to keep her as warm as possible until the doctor gets here."

Minutes felt like hours as they waited for

Levi and the doctor to arrive. Isaac never took his eyes off Mary, his heart aching with fear and desperation. He kept murmuring to her, telling her stories of Grace, of their early days together, anything to keep her tethered to the world.

Finally, the door burst open and Levi entered followed closely by Dr. Stoltzfus. The doctor, an elderly man with a kind face, immediately took charge, assessing Mary's condition with practiced efficiency.

"She's suffering from hypothermia," Dr. Stoltzfus informed them gravely. "We need to get her body temperature up gradually and carefully."

He instructed Isaac and Hannah on what to do, and together they worked to warm Mary, rubbing her limbs, changing out the hot water bottles, and feeding her small sips of warm broth. Isaac watched her every tiny movement, praying silently for her recovery.

Hours passed, and slowly, Mary's color began to return. Her breathing steadied, and the stiffness in her limbs started to ease.

Isaac watched Mary intently, his anxiety not subsiding as the minutes ticked by without her fully waking up.

"Mary?" he pressed. "Mary, can you hear me?"

He turned to Dr. Stoltzfus, his voice laced with desperation. "Why isn't she waking up, Doctor? What's wrong?"

Dr. Stoltzfus leaned in to check Mary's pupils, his brow furrowing in concern. "There's a bump on her head. She may have a concussion. It's likely that she fell and hit her head out in the park, and that's why she lay exposed to the elements."

Isaac's heart skittered in alarm. "What can we do to help her?"

Dr. Stoltzfus shook his head slowly. "There's not much we can do right now, Isaac. We need to let her rest and monitor her closely. If she doesn't show signs of improvement soon, then we'll need to take further measures. For now, keep her warm and try to be patient. I'll return later to check on her."

Isaac felt a wave of helplessness wash over him as Dr. Stoltzfus gathered his things and prepared to leave.

"*Danki*, Doctor," he murmured though the words felt hollow.

As the doctor left, closing the door softly behind him, Isaac turned his attention back to

Mary, his heart aching.

The day passed by painstakingly slowly. Isaac stayed by Mary's side, holding her hand and whispering words of comfort though he wasn't sure she could hear him. A heavy silence hung over the house, broken only by the occasional crackling of the fire.

Isaac was dimly aware of Hannah and Levi in the background. Hannah brought him tea and offered words of encouragement, but everything was dulled and void of color—as though he were trapped in a fog of fear.

"Isaac," Hannah prompted softly at one point, placing a cup of tea beside him. "You need to take care of yourself. Drink this, please."

He nodded absently, his eyes never leaving Mary's face.

The hours dragged on. Isaac prayed fervently, asking for strength and pleading for Mary's recovery.

As the light outside began to fade with the sun's dip below the horizon, Dr. Stoltzfus returned, bringing with him a renewed sense of hope. He checked Mary's condition carefully; after a thorough examination, he looked up at Isaac's expectant gaze.

"She's stable but still unresponsive," Dr. Stoltzfus said quietly. "Her pulse is stronger, which is a *gut* sign. We need to continue monitoring her. If she doesn't wake up by morning, we'll consider other options."

Isaac nodded, his heart heavy but clinging to the sliver of hope.

Dr. Stoltzfus offered a reassuring smile. "You're doing everything right, Isaac. Just keep her warm and comfortable. I'll be back first thing in the morning."

As the doctor left, Isaac settled back into his vigil, the emotional turmoil of the day pressing down on him. He was exhausted, but he refused to leave Mary's side.

Hannah and Levi continued their quiet support, understanding the depth of Isaac's worry. Hannah brought Isaac another cup of tea, but he barely noticed. His entire world was focused on the woman lying in front of him, the love of his life, the mother of his child.

As the night wore on, though Isaac felt exhaustion tugging at his eyelids, he refused to leave Mary's side. Just as dawn's rays began to filter through the windows, Isaac felt a faint movement in Mary's hand.

"Mary?" Isaac whispered, leaning closer.

Mary's eyes fluttered open, and she looked around in confusion. "Where am I?" she asked weakly, her voice barely above a whisper.

"You're home, Mary," Isaac said gently, relief flooding his voice. "You're safe."

Mary's eyes met his, her pain evident in her expression. "It hurts, Isaac. Everywhere."

"I know," he replied softly, stroking her face tenderly. "Just rest now. You're going to be okay."

Mary nodded slightly, her eyes heavy with exhaustion. As she drifted back to sleep, Isaac continued to stroke her face, his touch gentle and reassuring. He stayed beside her, finally giving in to his own exhaustion. He leaned back in the chair, still holding her hand, and allowed himself to doze off.

A few hours later, Isaac was jolted awake by Mary suddenly twitching. Her body jerked, and her face was pale but balmy, covered in a sheen of sweat. He reached out, feeling her forehead and realizing she was burning with a fever.

"Mary?" he called softly, trying to rouse her. "Mary, can you hear me?"

Mary's eyes opened, but they were unfocused and glassy. She muttered incoherently, her words barely making sense. "Grace...Grace is waiting for me."

Isaac's heart clenched with fear. "*Nee*, Mary. Stay with me. Don't go. Stay with me."

He turned his head to the door.

"Hannah, Levi, we need the doctor again. She's burning up, and she's not making sense."

They appeared in the doorway, their faces pale with apprehension.

"I'll go fetch Dr. Stoltzfus," said Hannah.

Levi immediately added, "I'll go with you."

Isaac watched as they hurried out the door, his mind racing. He turned back to Mary, taking her hand in his and squeezing it gently. "Please, Mary, stay with me. I need you."

Mary's eyes flickered open again, her expression one of pain and confusion. She continued to mutter Grace's name, her words breaking Isaac's heart. He stroked her face, the action soothing but his mind still filled with fear.

He stayed by Mary's side, praying silently for the doctor's swift arrival. He couldn't lose her —not now, not after everything they had been through.

Finally, the door burst open, and Dr. Stoltzfus rushed in with Hannah and Levi hot on his heels.

The doctor quickly assessed Mary's condition; his serious expression was not reassuring.

"She's developed a high fever," Dr. Stoltzfus said, his voice calm but with a sense of urgency. "We need to cool her down and bring the fever under control."

Under the doctor's guidance, they worked quickly to cool Mary's core temperature using cold compresses and fanning her gently. Isaac followed every instruction, his hands trembling but determined. He kept talking to Mary, his voice steady and soothing, urging her to stay with him.

Hours passed, and slowly, the fever began to break. Mary's twitching subsided, and her breathing became more even. Dr. Stoltzfus nodded, his concerned expression easing slightly.

"She's responding," he said in reassurance. "But she's still very weak."

Isaac nodded, relief flooding through him. "Is she going to be okay?"

Dr. Stoltzfus hesitated. "She's not out of the woods yet, I'm afraid. We'll need to keep her under close observation."

Isaac turned to Mary again, a lump

thickening his throat.

"Call me if the fever returns," the doctor instructed. "Otherwise, I will be back this evening to check on her."

"*Danki*, Doctor," said Hannah.

After the doctor had left, Isaac turned to Hannah.

"Will you sit with her for a bit?" he asked. "I need to get some air."

"Of course," replied Hannah.

Isaac rose and hurried from the room and out the back door. As he stepped outside, the cold air stung his lungs as he inhaled. His heart raced, and his thoughts were a tangled mess of fear and despair.

Why was this happening? What had they done to deserve this? He began to pace back and forth, his hands clenching and unclenching at his sides. Every step seemed to echo the tumult inside him, each breath a struggle against the panic threatening to overwhelm him.

"Isaac."

He turned to see Levi standing nearby. He walked over to him, his steps measured and steady.

"It's going to be okay," Levi reassured gently.

Isaac felt a surge of frustration and despair. "How do you know?" he challenged, his voice breaking. "How can you say that when everything is falling apart?"

Levi took a step forward, his gaze unwavering. "I don't know how things will turn out, Isaac. But I believe *Gott* is *gut* and that He is able to bring Mary through this. But if He doesn't, He is still *gut* and has a higher purpose that we may not come to understand this side of heaven. *Gott* is *gut,* Isaac. We have to hold onto that, especially when things seem darkest."

Isaac felt the fight drain out of him. He deflated, shaking his head. "I know that. But I can't lose her, Levi. I just can't."

Levi placed a comforting hand on Isaac's shoulder, his grip firm and reassuring. "You're not alone in this, Isaac. We're all here for you. For both of you. Mary is strong, and we're trusting God she'll rally. We know you'll get through this, come what may."

Isaac took a deep breath, trying to steady himself. He looked into Levi's eyes and saw the sincerity, the unwavering support.

And just like that, an invisible mantle of calmness settled over Isaac; the chaos in his mind eased. He took another deep breath, the cool air filling his lungs and clearing his head.

"Let's go back inside," Isaac said, his voice steadier. "I need to be with her."

Together, they walked back into the house. The warmth of the room enveloped them, and Isaac felt a renewed sense of faith and hope as he returned to Mary's side. He took her hand in his, and the familiar touch grounded him. Mary stirred slightly, her face still pale but peaceful in sleep.

"Please, *Gott*," Isaac whispered. "Please let my Mary *kumm* back to me."

Chapter Nine

Hannah stood in the kitchen, staring out the window as her thoughts drifted to Mary and Isaac. It was two days since they found Mary in the park, and while her fever had not returned, she was still very weak. She had no appetite, refused food, and hardly drank, which added to the already tremendous concern. It wasn't only Mary that Hannah was worried about but Isaac, too. He refused to leave Mary's side and hardly slept a wink. The lines of exhaustion etched deeper into his face with each passing hour. Hannah wished she could do more to help.

The sound of the back door opening pulled Hannah from her thoughts. She turned to see Levi stepping in, his head and shoulders dusted with snow. He walked over to the stove to warm his hands.

"How are things going?" Levi asked, his voice gentle but filled with concern.

Hannah sighed, shaking her head. "*Nee* change."

Levi nodded, his brow furrowed.

"Lunch is ready," Hannah said, gesturing to the table.

Levi turned and joined Hannah at the table, where she served him a bowl of stew and some fresh bread. For a moment, neither of them spoke.

"How are things going in the workshop?" she eventually asked, trying to keep the conversation light.

Levi offered a small reassuring smile. "I'm confident I can finish the orders in time."

"That's *gut*."

They fell silent again as Hannah looked down at the bowl of soup in front of her, but she had no appetite.

Then, to her surprise, Levi leaned across the table and took her hand.

"It will be okay," he said softly, his eyes meeting hers.

Her heart raced at his touch. But before she could say anything, Isaac stepped into the kitchen.

Hannah quickly pulled her hand back, her voice filled with concern. "Is everything all right? Is it Mary?"

Isaac shook his head, his expression weary.

"Do you want some lunch?" Hannah offered, hoping to give him some strength.

Isaac shook his head. "I'm not hungry."

"I am making *gut* progress with the orders," Levi offered. "We'll have them finished in time."

But Isaac seemed to hardly hear him. He nodded absently before turning and leaving the kitchen again.

Hannah and Levi exchanged a worried glance. After Levi finished his lunch, he returned to the workshop, and Hannah began to clear the table. As she did, she heard the faint sound of hammering from the workshop, and her mind drifted to thoughts of Levi. He had been so helpful over the last couple of days, stepping in to take over the Christmas orders so Isaac could be with Mary. His kindness and attentiveness had not gone unnoticed. He was always there, ready to lend a hand or offer a reassuring word.

Despite the brief time they had known each other, Hannah felt a deep connection with Levi. She was drawn to his steady presence, his faith, and the quiet strength he exuded. There was something about the way he listened, genuinely listened, and the way he seemed to understand her without needing many words. His gentle smile and the warmth in his eyes had become a source of comfort for her.

Hannah had never expected to feel this way about someone she had only recently met. It was a strange, exciting, and somewhat scary feeling. She found herself looking forward to their conversations, enjoying the ease with which they talked about anything and everything.

The memory of Levi leaning across the table to take her hand resurfaced, causing her heart to skip a beat. The touch was brief, but it had left a lasting impression. In that moment, she had felt a flicker of hope, a sense that maybe, just maybe, there could be something more between them.

After she finished the washing up, Hannah went to check on Isaac and Mary. She found Isaac still by Mary's side, holding her hand and whispering words of comfort.

As she made her way back to the kitchen, a

knock sounded at the door.

Hannah opened the door, expecting to see Dr. Stoltzfus. Instead, she found herself face-to-face with a pretty young woman about her own age. The woman smiled politely though she looked slightly uncertain.

"*Gude daag*," said Hannah, her brow furrowing slightly. "Can I help you?"

The young woman nodded. "*Ya*, I'm looking for Levi. Rachel told me I could find him here."

Hannah's frown deepened. "And who are you, if I may ask?"

"I'm Emma Lapp, Levi's fiancée."

The very ground shifted beneath Hannah's feet. She was absolutely shocked, her mind struggling to process what she had just heard.

"H-his f-fiancée?" she stammered.

"*Ya*," said Emma. "Is he here?"

Hannah's thoughts whipped through her mind in a whirlwind of confusion and hurt. Why hadn't Levi mentioned he was getting married? She felt a sudden, sharp pang of foolishness, her feelings for Levi seeming naïve and misplaced in light of this new information.

"He's...he's in the workshop out back," Hannah finally managed, stumbling over her words. "I'll show you."

She led Emma through the house, her mind racing. Each step felt heavy, her heart aching.

"Just through there," she said, pointing, her voice barely above a whisper.

Emma gave her a grateful smile.

Hannah watched as Emma made her way to the workshop, feeling a mix of emotions that she couldn't quite detangle. Did she misinterpret Levi's kindness and attention? The connection she had felt with him now seemed like a cruel joke.

Hannah turned back into the house, her steps slow and her heart heavy. She tried to focus on the tasks at hand, but her mind kept drifting back to the encounter with Emma at the door, the moment the bottom of her world had dropped out from beneath her.

She returned to the kitchen, her hands trembling slightly as she resumed cleaning up. She needed to stay focused, especially with Mary and Isaac going through so much. But it was difficult to push away or compartmentalize the hurt and confusion.

As she scrubbed a stubborn spot on the counter, she heard voices drifting in from the workshop. Emma and Levi were talking, but she couldn't make out the words.

Just then, another knock sounded at the door.

"Who could this be?" Hannah wondered aloud.

She wiped her hands on her apron and went to answer. Her father stood with Daniel at his side. Hannah forced a smile though her heart wasn't in it.

"*Vadder*. Daniel," she greeted.

Her father nodded, his expression serious but kind. "*Gude daag*, Hannah. I've *kumm* to pray with Isaac and Mary, and Daniel wanted to accompany me."

Hannah nodded. "Of course. Please, *kumm* in."

As they stepped inside, Daniel's hopeful expression as his eyes met hers made her stomach churn. She didn't have the energy to deal with him, but under her father's watchful gaze, Hannah felt obliged to invite Daniel to join her for tea.

A short while later, they sat at the kitchen table, the atmosphere awkward and heavy with unspoken words. As Hannah poured the tea, they saw Levi through the window, walking Emma out through the back garden.

Daniel's eyes narrowed. "Who is she?" he asked, nodding towards the window.

Hannah replied impassively, "That's Emma Lapp, Levi's fiancée."

Daniel's face lit up as his gaze remained on the couple, clearly pleased by this revelation. He leaned forward in his seat and redirected his gaze to Hannah. "I know this might not be the best time…" he began.

Hannah's stomach immediately knotted. She did not want to have this conversation.

"But now that your *vadder's* agreed that we make a good match, we should start courting officially. I think it's time," he finished.

Hannah said nothing. She wanted to protest, to tell Daniel that her heart wasn't in it, but the actuality of Levi's engagement was unavoidable. Maybe her father was right; she wasn't getting any younger. Maybe it was time to move forward —even if her heart wasn't fully in it.

She took a deep breath and nodded. "All right, Daniel," she conceded. "We can start courting."

Daniel's face broke into a broad smile, and

before she could react, he stood and pulled her into a hug. "This is *wunderbaar*, Hannah. You won't regret it."

At that very moment, the back door opened, and Levi walked in, his eyes widening as he took in the scene. Hannah felt a pang of guilt and sorrow at the evident hurt on his face. She pulled away from Daniel, feeling more conflicted than ever.

Levi's voice was strained as he spoke. "Is everything all right in here?"

Daniel, still beaming, gushed proudly, "Everything is more than all right. Hannah and I just agreed to start courting officially."

Levi stiffened as his gaze met Hannah's, and she read his pain in them.

"Is that right?" he asked.

"*Ya*," replied Hannah.

Levi looked as if he wanted to say something else, but instead, he just nodded curtly. "Congratulations," he said, his voice hollow.

Hannah wanted to reach out to him, to explain that he was already spoken for so she felt she had no other choice, but the words wouldn't come. She watched as Levi turned and left the room, the door closing softly behind him.

Despite the fact that Levi was engaged and she was annoyed at herself for having thought she could have something with him that was never even a possibility, Hannah felt a sense of loss she had not fully expected.

Daniel returned to his seat, blind to the tension in the room. "This is going to be great, Hannah. I can feel it."

Hannah forced another smile, but inside, her heart was breaking. She knew she was making the pragmatic choice, the choice everyone expected her to make. But as she sat there sipping her tea, she mourned the fact she had not only lost a potential spouse in Levi but also his friendship.

Hannah stood in the doorway of Mary and Isaac's bedroom. Dr. Stoltzfus was leaning over Mary as he pressed his stethoscope to her chest. Hannah glanced at Isaac seated at Mary's bedside, his face etched with worry and fatigue.

A short while later, Dr. Stoltzfus stood up and turned to them, his expression serious but calm.

"Mary is still stable, but if she doesn't wake up in the next twelve hours, I would recommend taking her to the hospital in the city. She might need more intensive care than we can provide here."

Isaac's face tightened as he nodded stiffly. "*Danki*, Doctor," he said quietly.

Dr. Stoltzfus began to gather his things and then headed to the door. Hannah stepped aside to allow him past.

"*Gude nacht*," he said with a nod.

"*Gude nacht,* Doctor," Hannah replied.

As the front door closed behind Dr. Stoltzfus, Isaac turned to Hannah, his eyes holding a mixture of gratitude and exhaustion.

"Hannah, you should go home. There's nothing more you can do here," Isaac said gently.

Hannah shook her head, determined. "I want to stay. I can help."

Isaac's expression softened, but he remained firm. "I appreciate everything you've done, but I need some time alone with Mary. Please, go home and rest. You've done more than enough."

Hannah felt a pang of sadness but understood Isaac's need for privacy. "All right, Isaac. If you need anything, please let me know."

Isaac nodded.

"I will be back in the morning," Hannah assured him.

With a heavy heart, she left the house, her mind still reeling from the day's events. She hadn't seen Levi since that afternoon when he walked in on her and Daniel in the kitchen. The memory of the hurt in his eyes haunted her, and she longed to talk about it, to defend her decision in light of him being engaged—but most of all, to repair their friendship.

As she walked towards the workshop, she hesitated outside the door, willing herself to go inside and talk to Levi. She stood there, gathering her courage, but after everything that had happened, it all just felt like too much. She couldn't face him just then, not with her emotions so raw and tangled.

Sighing deeply, Hannah turned away and headed home. The walk was long and lonely, her thoughts swirling with confusion and regret.

When she finally reached her house, the warmth inside did little to soothe her troubled heart. She sank into a chair, feeling the exhaustion of the day settle over her. She knew she had made the choice that was expected of her, especially given that she wasn't getting any younger and that Levi's heart was already promised, but it was still difficult. Her mind kept drifting back to Levi, to the connection they had shared, and to the possibility of what might have been.

Chapter Ten

L evi stood in the workshop, the comfortingly familiar scents of wood and sawdust filling the air. He looked around at the neatly stacked Christmas orders, each one a testament to the hard work he had put in over the past few days. Yet, despite the completion of the orders, there was no sense of satisfaction, only a gnawing emptiness in the pit of his stomach. The events of the day had left him feeling unsettled and lost.

He was just about to close up the workshop for the night when the door opened. He turned to see Isaac standing there, looking surprised to find him still working.

"Levi, you're still here?"

"*Ya*, I was just finishing up," Levi replied,

forcing a small smile. "How's Mary?"

Isaac sighed, his shoulders sagging. "The doctor said if she doesn't wake up by morning, we should take her to the hospital in the city."

"I'm so sorry, Isaac. I wish there was more I could do."

Isaac nodded, his eyes reflecting the same helplessness.

Isaac looked at Levi, his gaze probing. "Are *you* all right?" he asked.

"*Ach,* it's nothing. I don't want to bother you with it, especially with everything that's going on with Mary."

Isaac's expression softened. "I could use the distraction, honestly."

Levi hesitated, then nodded. They both sat down beside the workbench. He took a deep breath.

"Emma came to see me today," he said, his voice low.

Isaac raised an eyebrow. "Emma?"

"She and I were supposed to marry," Levi explained.

"And she came here? To Willowvale?"

Levi nodded. "At one point she was everything I thought I wanted. We had our lives planned out, but after my *eldre* died, something changed in me. I realized that I was making decisions based on what I thought I should do rather than what I really wanted. So, I broke it off. I didn't want to hurt her, but I couldn't go through with it knowing my heart wasn't in it."

Isaac listened intently, his eyes filled with empathy. "So, what did she want?"

"She came to tell me she misses me," Levi explained. "And that she's willing to move to Willowvale if I'm willing to give us a second chance."

Isaac frowned slightly. "And how do you feel about that?"

Levi sighed, running a hand through his hair. "I'm not sure. Seeing her brought back a lot of memories..."

His voice trailed off as he shook his head. "I mean, how does anyone know who they are supposed to marry? How can one be sure about what it feels like to be in love and that they've found the person they want to spend the rest of their lives with?"

Isaac leaned back. "I asked myself those same questions once. When I met Mary, I was young and unsure about what the future would hold.

But there were moments, little moments, that made me realize she was the one."

Levi listened intently, absorbing Isaac's words.

"For me, it was the way Mary smiled, the way she laughed, and how she always knew how to comfort me when I was down," Isaac continued. "We haven't always had it easy. There were times we struggled, especially when we thought we couldn't have *kinner*. But through it all, Mary was my rock. I realized that love isn't just about the *gut* times. It's about finding someone who stands by you during the hard times, who lifts you up when you're at your lowest."

Levi nodded slowly as his thoughts turned to Hannah. He recalled the warmth of her smile and the way she always seemed to understand him without needing many words. He thought about how she had been there for Mary and Isaac and how she had shown strength and compassion in the face of adversity.

"When you're with the right person, you just feel it," Isaac said. "It's not always fireworks and grand gestures. Sometimes it's the quiet moments, the simple acts of kindness and understanding. It's the feeling that no matter what happens, you'll face it together."

Levi looked up, meeting Isaac's gaze. "But what if you're unsure? What if you're afraid of making the wrong choice?"

Isaac smiled gently. "It's natural to feel unsure. But trust your heart. When you look at this person, ask yourself: Does she make you want to be a better person? Do you feel at peace when you're with her? Do you miss her when she's not around?"

Levi said nothing as Isaac reached over and squeezed his shoulder.

"Remember that it's okay to be unsure. Just be honest with yourself and with those you care about."

"Emma's staying with a distant cousin in town for a few days," Levi said. "I told her I needed time to think about it."

Isaac nodded. "Well, you will make the right decision."

Levi nodded with a newfound resolve. He knew he had to talk to Hannah, to explain everything and to be honest about his feelings. It was the only way he could be sure of what he wanted.

"Well, I'm going to bed," said Isaac.

"*Guder owed*, Isaac. And *danki*."

Isaac smiled at him before he got up and left Levi alone with his thoughts.

A short while later, Levi left the workshop and headed back towards Rachel's house. With each step, he felt a growing sense of purpose.

As he turned the street, Levi noticed a plume of smoke rising in the distance, its dark tendrils curling ominously into the sky.

As he drew nearer and arrived at the scene, the sight before him sent a shiver of fear straight to his core. The community building was fully engulfed in flames, the fire roaring with a terrifying intensity as it devoured the wooden structure. The heat was overwhelming, radiating outwards in waves that seemed to scorch the very air. The sound of crackling wood was deafening, punctuated by sharp pops and groans as parts of the building collapsed in on itself.

All around him, townspeople were shouting. Their voices were strained with desperation as they formed lines to pass buckets of water, doing everything they could to battle the relentless blaze. But Levi barely registered any of it. He stood rooted to the spot, his breath catching in his throat, his body frozen in place.

Suddenly, the scene before him began to blur and shift, and Levi's mind was pulled back to another night, one he had tried so hard to forget. He was no longer in Willowvale; he was back home, standing in front of his own family's house as it burned. The flames had been just as fierce, just as unforgiving, and he had been just as helpless.

He remembered the thick, acrid smoke that had filled his lungs, choking him as he struggled to breathe. The heat had been unbearable, searing his skin as he fought to make it to safety. He had managed to escape, stumbling out into the cool night air, gasping for breath. But when he turned back, desperate to see if his parents were behind him, all he had seen was the fire raging and consuming everything in its path.

They hadn't made it out. The realization had hit him with the force of a hammer, knocking the very breath from his lungs and sending him to his knees. The screams of neighbors, the wailing of sirens—all of it had faded into the background as he crumpled to the ground, overcome with grief and guilt. He survived, but his parents didn't, and that knowledge had haunted him every day since.

Now, standing in front of the burning community building in Willowvale, that same panic gripped Levi once again. His chest tightened, and his breath came in short, shallow gasps as the memories surged up, suffocating him. The world around him seemed to close in, and the roar of the flames drowned out everything else until all he could hear was the pounding of his own heart in his ears.

He couldn't move, couldn't think. All he could do was stand there, paralyzed. The flames before him melded with the ones from his past, merging into a single, terrifying inferno that threatened to swallow him whole.

Levi's vision blurred as his eyes filled with tears, the sting of smoke adding to the burn. His knees trembled, and he felt himself starting to sink to the ground, just as he had that night so many months ago. The sense of helplessness was overwhelming, choking him as he struggled to draw air into his lungs. His hands clenched into fists at his sides, his nails digging into his palms as he fought to keep himself grounded in the present.

But the past was too strong, the memories

too vivid. His mind was filled with images of his parents—his mother's kind smile, his father's reassuring presence—both of them lost to the fire that destroyed his home and shattered his life. He had been powerless then, and he felt just as powerless now.

Just as it seemed like the panic would consume him, a voice broke through the haze, cutting through the noise and the fear like a lifeline.

"Levi!" The voice was urgent, filled with concern, and it pulled him back to the present with a jolt.

Levi blinked, his vision clearing as he looked around, trying to locate the source of the voice. His heart was still racing, his breath still coming in ragged gasps, but he could see again. He was in Willowvale, not back home. This wasn't his family's house, and this wasn't the same fire.

"Levi!" The voice came again, closer this time, and Levi finally registered the face in front of him. It was Conrad, his brother-in-law, his expression filled with worry as he reached out to grab Levi's arm, shaking him gently. "Levi, snap out of it! We need your help!"

The touch, the familiarity of Conrad's voice,

grounded Levi in reality. He forced himself to focus, to push back the memories that had threatened to drag him under. With a Herculean effort, he took a deep breath, feeling the air rush into his lungs, and forced himself to nod.

"I-I'm here," Levi stammered, his voice trembling as he tried to regain control. "What... what do you need me to do?"

Conrad didn't hesitate. "We need to clear a path around the building to stop the fire from spreading to the other houses. Grab an ax and help us cut down anything flammable."

Levi nodded again, the instructions giving him something to focus on, something with which to anchor himself to the present. He could still feel the panic lurking at the edges of his mind, but he tamped it down, determined not to let it take over again.

He followed Conrad's lead, grabbing an ax from a nearby cart and joining the other men as they worked to cut down the bushes and trees around the community building, anything that could fuel the fire and spread it further. His hands shook as he swung the ax, but with each stroke, he felt a little more in control, a little more grounded.

As the flames continued to rage behind him, Levi forced himself to focus on the task at hand, each swing of the ax a step further away from the darkness of his past.

Around him, more and more buckets of water were being passed along a human chain from the nearby well, their contents thrown onto the flames in a desperate attempt to quell the fire.

"Keep it moving!" Bishop Weaver shouted, his voice barely audible over the roar of the fire. "Don't let it spread!"

Levi's muscles burned with the effort, but he didn't slow down. Sweat mingled with soot on his face, and his hands grew raw from the friction of the ax. The heat was almost unbearable, and the flames cast an eerie, flickering light on the determined faces of the townspeople.

The acrid smell of burning wood and smoke was thick in the air. Levi could taste the bitterness of it on his tongue, and he fought to keep his eyes open despite the stinging pain. The fire seemed relentless, each bucket of water hissing in defeat as it hit the flames, sending up plumes of steam.

"Over here! We need more water!" Mr. Yoder called from the other side of the building, and Levi, along with a few others, shifted their efforts to the new area, hoping to contain the blaze.

The process was grueling, a test of endurance and resolve. Levi felt his strength waning but pushed through, driven by the collective determination of the community.

"Grab a bucket, Levi," Conrad called.

Gradually, their efforts began to pay off. The flames, once towering and fierce, started to diminish, their roar growing quieter as the water proved to be the stronger opponent. The smoke still billowed, but it was less dense, less suffocating. Levi's arms ached, and his lungs burned, but he kept going, knowing that every drop of water brought them closer to saving what remained.

"Keep it up! We're almost there!" Bishop Weaver encouraged, and Levi felt a renewed surge of energy.

Finally, after what felt like hours but was likely only minutes, the flames were brought under control. The fire was reduced to smoldering embers, the charred remains of the building still smoking but no longer threatening to spread. The townspeople, covered in soot and sweat, stood back, panting and exhausted but relieved.

Levi dropped the empty bucket and wiped his forehead with the back of his hand, looking around at the weary but triumphant faces of his neighbors. The community had come together in their time of need, and despite the damage, they managed to save a part of the building.

"Anyone know what happened?" Levi asked, his voice still hoarse from the smoke.

Conrad shook his head, wiping sweat and soot from his brow. "No one knows for sure. Maybe a lamp got knocked over or something else went wrong. It all happened so fast."

Levi nodded, the gravity of the situation sinking in. Before they could discuss it further, Bishop Weaver's voice rose above the murmur of the crowd. The bishop stood on a small rise, addressing the townspeople who had gathered. Levi looked around for Hannah, but she was nowhere to be seen.

"*Danki* all for your efforts tonight," Bishop Weaver began, tone one of gratitude and resolve. "You have shown the strength of our *gmay*.

Please, go home and get some rest. Those who are able and willing, please meet back here in the morning. We will discuss the rebuilding of our community center and how to move forward."

The crowd began to disperse, weary but united in their determination to rebuild. Levi and Conrad made their way home, their steps heavy with fatigue. When they reached the house, Rachel was waiting for them at the door, her face pale with worry.

"Thank goodness you're both all right," she exclaimed, rushing to hug them both tightly.

Levi and Conrad embraced her, their own relief mingling with hers.

"We're fine, Rachel," Conrad reassured her. "The fire is out, and the community center is mostly saved."

Rachel pulled back, her eyes scanning their faces. "*Kumm* inside, both of you. I've made some hot cocoa. You need to warm up and rest."

They entered the warm, welcoming kitchen, the delicious smell of cocoa mingling with the lingering smokey scent on their clothes and hair. Rachel quickly poured them steaming mugs, and they sat around the table, the warmth of the cocoa infusing heat into their chilled bodies.

Levi took a sip, savoring the comforting taste.

"I'm going to volunteer to help with the rebuilding," he announced. "Now that the *Grischtdaag* orders are complete, I have the time."

Conrad nodded, his expression one of approval. "I'll go with you. We're going to need all hands on deck."

As they finished their cocoa and their bodies warmed, the exhaustion from the day's events began to catch up with them. A round of yawns passed amongst the trio. Rachel stood and started gathering the empty mugs. "Let's all get some rest. Tomorrow is going to be a long day."

Levi and Conrad nodded without argument, rising from the table. As Levi neared the door, Rachel asked, "Are you sure you're all right?"

"I just froze," Levi murmured, shaking his head. "When I saw the fire, I couldn't move, think, or breathe. If Conrad hadn't been there..."

Rachel walked up to her brother and placed a hand gently on his arm.

"It's understandable," she said softly. "After what you went through."

Levi swallowed and nodded.

"Get some rest," Rachel counseled. "Things

always look better in the morning."

As Levi headed to his room, he couldn't help but think of Hannah, a pang of longing to see her, to talk to her, piercing him as he wondered how she was coping with everything.

The next morning, Levi and Conrad walked together to the meeting. The sky was clear, the crisp morning air invigorating. As they approached the site, Levi saw the townspeople milling around, exchanging greetings and discussing the fire.

Levi's eyes were immediately drawn to Hannah in the crowd, who was busy handing out cinnamon rolls to the men, her smile bright and warm. His heart skipped a beat at the sight of her, the ache from the previous day's revelation still fresh. He started to make his way toward her, wanting to speak with her, but stopped when he saw Daniel standing beside her. Daniel took a cinnamon roll from her, and his fingers brushed tenderly against hers. The intimate gesture made Levi's stomach churn with jealousy and regret.

Just then, Bishop Weaver called for attention, his authoritative voice cutting through the chatter. The crowd's conversations abated as they turned to face him.

"*Danki* all for coming, especially with *Grischtdaag* just around the corner," he began. "Last night was a stark reminder of the importance of our *gmay* and the strength we draw from each other. The community building serves as a place of charity and goodwill, particularly during this time of year. It's where we gather to help those less fortunate, and it's crucial that we rebuild it as quickly as possible."

The bishop's words were met with nods and murmurs of agreement. He continued, "As most of you know, our town carpenter, Isaac Fisher, could not be here today due to his *fraa's* illness. While we keep them in our prayers, this does mean that we need someone to step forward and lead this rebuilding effort."

Everyone looked around, waiting for someone to volunteer. Conrad nudged Levi gently.

Levi took a deep breath as he stepped forward. "I know I'm new to Willowvale, but my *vadder* was a carpenter, and I've learned the skills of the trade. I would be honored to help lead the rebuilding effort."

"He's been working with Mr. Fisher," Conrad added. "He helped to complete all the *Grischtdaag* orders."

Murmurs of surprise and approval rippled through the group.

The bishop looked hesitant for a brief moment before nodding in approval. "*Danki*. Your willingness to step up is greatly appreciated, Mr. Miller."

Levi chanced a glance at Hannah, who met his eye; however, the moment was interrupted by Daniel, who stepped closer to her, placing a protective hand on her shoulder.

Bishop Weaver continued, outlining the plan for the rebuilding process. "We'll start with clearing the debris and salvaging whatever we can. Then, we'll begin reconstruction. I ask everyone who is able to lend a hand to please do so. We need all the help we can get."

The townspeople nodded, their faces set with resolve.

"I'll now hand over the reins to Mr. Miller," Bishop Weaver ended, nodding in Levi's direction.

Levi took charge, directing the community members as they began clearing the debris and salvaging what they could from the charred remains of the community building.

"Careful with those beams," Levi called out to a group of men lifting a partially burned support beam. "We might be able to use some of this wood for the new structure."

As the men carefully carried the beam to a salvage pile, Levi moved among the workers, checking on their progress and offering assistance where needed. He was grateful for the opportunity to put his skills to use and felt a sense of purpose in leading the effort.

But even as he focused on the task at hand, Levi couldn't help but keep half an eye on Hannah. She was moving through the crowd, helping where she could and offering smiles and words of encouragement to everyone. Despite the soot smudging her face and the exhaustion in her eyes, to him, she looked as radiant as ever. Levi's heart ached to talk to her, to explain everything, but Daniel was constantly by her side, his protective presence making it difficult for Levi to approach her.

Levi watched as Hannah handed out water

to the workers, her gentle touch and kind words lifting their spirits. She laughed at something one of the older men said, and her eyes crinkled at the corners. A pang of longing coursed through Levi; he wanted to be the one making her laugh, the one standing by her side.

"Levi, what should we do with these bricks?" a voice interrupted his thoughts. He turned to see a young man holding a couple of bricks, their edges blackened by the fire.

"Stack them over there," Levi instructed, pointing to a corner where they were gathering usable materials. "We'll see if we can clean them up and use them again."

The young man nodded and carried the bricks to the designated area. Levi took a deep breath, refocusing on the work. He couldn't afford to be distracted, not with so much at stake. The community was depending on him, and he needed to stay focused.

As the hours passed, the pile of salvaged materials grew. Beams, bricks, and other structural elements that could be repurposed were carefully set aside. The debris was gradually cleared, revealing the foundations of the old building.

Levi continued to monitor the progress while his mind was constantly swirling with plans and calculations. Yet, his eyes frequently strayed to Hannah. Each time he saw her, regret and frustration welled up in him. He knew he had to talk to her, but Daniel's constant presence made it virtually impossible.

Finally, Levi saw an opportunity when Daniel stepped away to speak with Bishop Weaver. Levi seized the moment, approaching Hannah as she handed out more water to the workers.

"Hannah," he called softly.

She turned to him, her expression momentarily brightening before a shadow of uncertainty crossed her face. "Levi," she replied, her voice gentle.

"I wanted to talk to you," Levi said, edging closer. "About yesterday..."

Before Levi could continue, Daniel returned, his expression wary. He stepped between them, his protective stance clear in intention. "Is everything all right here?"

Levi clenched his jaw, biting back the frustration boiling beneath the surface. "*Ya*, Daniel. I just wanted to speak with Hannah for a moment."

Daniel's eyes narrowed slightly, but he nodded. He stepped back, making sure, though, that he was still in earshot of their conversation.

Levi looked back at Hannah, his heart pounding. "Can we meet up and talk later when things have settled down?"

Hannah glanced between Levi and Daniel.

"All right, Levi. We can talk later."

Levi nodded, a small glimmer of hope igniting within him. With that, he stepped back, giving her space as Daniel resumed his position by her side. The moment was brief, but it was enough to give Levi a sense of encouragement. He returned to the task at hand with renewed determination, knowing that he would soon have the chance to clear the air with Hannah.

As the day wore on and the debris was slowly but surely cleared, Levi felt bolstered by a sense of achievement. The community was making progress, and despite the challenges, they were moving forward. And, most importantly, amidst the hard work, Levi held onto the hope that he could make things right with Hannah.

Chapter Eleven

Mary was in the park again, reveling in the familiar warmth of the sun on her face and the chirrups of birds singing in the trees. The grass was a vibrant green, and flowers bloomed in a riot of colors all around. Grace was there, her sweet laughter trilling through the air as they played. Mary's heart swelled with joy; her love for her daughter was so intense it was almost overwhelming. She kissed Grace's face, stroked her soft hair, and held her close, savoring every precious second.

They spun around in circles, with Grace's giggles ringing out in a childish symphony. Mary felt lighter than she had in a long time, her heart almost bursting with happiness. A piercing light suddenly blinded Mary. She squinted against it as her eyes struggled to adjust. Grace's small hands cupped either side of her face, and she looked into her daughter's eyes, seeing wisdom and understanding far beyond her years.

"It's time to wake up, *Maem*," Grace said softly, her voice carrying a gentle insistence.

Mary's heart clenched. "I want to stay with you, Grace."

Grace shook her head with a tender and knowing smile. "It's time to wake up."

Tears welled up in Mary's eyes. "I don't want to leave you."

Grace smiled again as she placed her small hand over Mary's heart, her touch warm and comforting. "I'm in here, with you always."

Mary burst into sobs with the pain of their separation cutting through her joy from but a moment before. "I miss you so much."

"I know, *Maem*," Grace said softly. "But you need to wake up now."

The world around them began to fade, and the bright light grew more intense. Grace's image started to blur, but her touch remained, solid and real. Mary clung to her, not wanting to let go, but Grace's voice echoed in her mind.

"Wake up, *Maem*."

With a jolt, Mary opened her eyes. The vividness of the dream faded, replaced by the dim light of her bedroom. She blinked, her vision adjusting, and saw Isaac sitting beside her, his head bowed in prayer. His hand held hers tightly, and the strain and exhaustion were etched into his features.

"Isaac," she whispered in a weak but steady voice.

Isaac's head shot up, his eyes wide with disbelief and hope. "Mary? Mary, you're awake!"

She nodded slowly. "It was Grace... She told me to wake up. To *kumm* back to you."

Tears filled Isaac's eyes, and he leaned forward to kiss her forehead gently. "We've all been so worried."

Mary squeezed his hand weakly, a sense of peace settling over her despite the lingering pain. "I saw her in my dream, Isaac. I know she's okay."

Isaac nodded, his voice choked with emotion as he leaned over and kissed her. "I was so worried I was going to lose you."

"It's okay," Mary said. "I'm here."

The front door opened and closed with a click, followed by the sound of footsteps approaching and then a gentle knock on the door. It creaked open, and Hannah stepped into the room.

Hannah's eyes widened in pleasant surprise, and a bright smile spread across her face at the sight of Mary awake and alert. "Mary!" she exclaimed, her voice filled with relief and joy. "You're awake!"

Mary managed a small smile, her heart warming at Hannah's happiness. "*Ya*, I'm awake," she said softly, her voice still slightly weak but steadier.

Hannah moved quickly to the bedside, and her eyes shone with unshed tears. "*Ach*, Mary, we've all been so worried about you," she said, reaching out to gently touch Mary's hand.

Isaac, who had been sitting quietly beside Mary, looked up at Hannah with gratitude in his eyes. "Would you mind fetching the doctor?" he asked. "We need to make sure Mary is okay."

"Of course," Hannah replied immediately. "I'll go right away."

She squeezed Mary's hand gently, then turned and left the room, her steps quick and purposeful as she hurried to find Dr. Stoltzfus. As she disappeared down the hallway, Mary's gaze lingered on the door before turning back to Isaac.

"She's been so kind, hasn't she?" Mary said softly, thinking of all the times Hannah had come by to help, to offer comfort, even when Mary was too lost in her own grief to accept it.

Isaac nodded, his expression tender. "She has. Hannah's been a blessing to us both."

Mary nodded in agreement, feeling a swell of gratitude for her friend. She could see now how much Hannah had tried to help, even when Mary pushed everyone away.

"She's been here almost every day," Isaac continued, his voice soft. "Checking on you, helping around the house...Levi, too."

Mary squeezed Isaac's hand. Her heart was full of appreciation for Hannah's unwavering support. "I'll have to thank her properly when I'm stronger," she said quietly, already thinking of how she could express her gratitude.

The room fell into silence for a while. But before long, they heard the front door open and close and then the sound of footsteps returning quickly down the hall. Hannah reappeared in the doorway, a little out of breath but smiling sunnily with Dr. Stoltzfus on her heels.

"*Gude mariye*, Mary," Dr. Stoltzfus greeted,

his voice warm and reassuring. "It's *gut* to see you awake."

"*Gude mariye,* Doctor," Mary replied softly as he pulled up a chair and sat beside her.

"Let's have a look at you," Dr. Stoltzfus said, gently taking her wrist to check her pulse.

He performed a thorough examination with careful and precise movements, listening to her heart, checking her breathing, and examining her eyes. Mary watched his face closely, searching for any sign of concern.

After a few moments, Dr. Stoltzfus leaned back with a small smile tugging at the corners of his mouth. "Well, Mary, you seem well," he announced. "You're weak, as expected, but you're out of the woods. Your heart is strong, and your vital signs are stable."

Isaac let out a breath as his hand tightened around Mary's. "*Danki*, Doctor."

Dr. Stoltzfus nodded, his expression pleased but still serious. "She'll need plenty of rest, and it's important that she starts taking in more fluids. Start off with broth and then gradually introduce thicker soup and then solids. Small, frequent meals will help rebuild her strength. Keep her warm and comfortable, and be patient with the recovery process. It will take time, but I'm confident she'll make a full recovery."

Mary's eyes filled with gratitude. "*Danki*, Dr. Stoltzfus."

He smiled gently at her, patting her hand. "*Gaern gschehne*, Mary. You've been through a lot, but you're strong. Just take things one day at a time."

With that, Dr. Stoltzfus stood up, nodding to Isaac and Hannah. "If anything changes or if you have any concerns, don't hesitate to call me. But for now, I think Mary's on the path to full recovery."

Isaac shook the doctor's hand firmly. "*Danki* again, Doctor. We appreciate everything you've done."

Dr. Stoltzfus gathered his things and headed toward the door.

"I'll give you two some time alone, but if you need anything, I'll be right outside," Hannah said softly.

Mary met Isaac's eyes, which were brimming with tenderness. For a moment, neither of them spoke. The room was quiet except for the soft sound of Isaac's breathing beside her. She could feel the warmth of his hand enveloping hers, grounding her, reminding her that she was alive.

"Isaac," she whispered, her voice hoarse but steady.

Isaac's eyes, shining with unshed tears, looked at her as though he couldn't believe she was really awake, really there with him. "Mary," he murmured, his voice thick with emotion. He squeezed her hand, his grip firm and reassuring as if he was afraid to let go.

"I was ready to go," Mary said softly, her voice breaking the silence that had settled between them. "I wanted to be with Grace."

A sob escaped Isaac's throat, raw and full of anguish. He leaned closer to her, his face crumpling. Mary reached up with her free hand, cupping his face tenderly, feeling the roughness of his unshaven jaw beneath her palm. Isaac nuzzled into her hand, his eyes closing as if her touch was the only thing keeping him from falling apart.

"But," Mary continued, her voice trembling, "I see that I don't want to leave you, Isaac. We still have so much to live for, so much to fight for."

Tears streamed down Isaac's cheeks, and he pressed her palm to his lips, his breath shuddering. "I was so scared, Mary. I thought I'd lost you."

Mary's heart ached at the depth of his pain, pain she had caused by retreating into her own sorrow. "I'm so sorry," she whispered, her voice filled with regret. "I'm so sorry for pushing you away, for shutting you out."

Isaac opened his eyes, his gaze locking with hers. There was so much in those eyes—love, pain, hope. He didn't say anything at first and just leaned into her hand, letting the warmth of her touch soothe him. "I understood," he finally said, his voice low and thick with emotion. "I understood why you needed to pull away. But I never stopped loving you, Mary. I never will."

Mary's eyes filled with tears as her chest tightened. "We're going to be okay, Isaac," she whispered, her thumb gently brushing away the tears from his cheek. "It's all going to be okay. We'll find a way through this, together."

Isaac nodded, leaning down to press his forehead against hers. "Together," he echoed, his voice a soft promise. "We'll get through this together."

They stayed like that for a while, the silence between them no longer heavy with unspoken fears but filled with the quiet comfort of understanding and shared strength. Mary felt a small fragile hope begin to take root in her heart, a hope that they could rebuild, that they could heal.

As she lay there holding Isaac's hand, she knew that the road ahead wouldn't be easy. But with Isaac by her side, she believed she could once again face life. Grace's memory would always be with them, a light in their darkest times. And in that moment, with Isaac's hand in hers, Mary experienced a fresh sense of purpose and a determination to live the life that God gave her with the man to whom she had made her lifelong vows.

"We're going to be okay," she whispered again, more to herself than to Isaac. But she believed it, and for the first time in as long as she could remember, Mary felt at peace.

A few days had passed, and Mary could feel herself growing stronger with each sunrise. It was a slow process—each step small but significant. She still tired easily, and there were times when her body felt weak, but something fundamental had shifted within her. It was as if she was living under the shadow of darkness for a long time, but now, finally, she had stepped into bright sunlight.

The grief that had once devoured her, pulling her into a downward spiral of misery, was still there, but it felt different. It was no longer an overpowering force, strangling her spirit. Rather, it had softened into something she could hold close to her heart, something that reminded her of the love she had for Grace without drowning in the sorrow. The memory of Grace was no longer something that caused her unbearable pain; it had become a reminder of the hope of the future.

Isaac was with Mary constantly, his attentiveness and presence a steady comfort. He had hardly left her side since she woke up, and Mary could feel the strength of their bond returning, perhaps even stronger than before, tempered by the fire of shared grief. They spent hours talking quietly, sometimes about Grace, sometimes about the future, and other times, they simply sat in companionable silence, finding peace in just being together.

One afternoon, as Mary sat in bed propped up by pillows and Isaac read aloud from the Bible, his voice a soothing rhythm in the quiet room, Mary reached out, taking his hand in hers. It was her instinctive gesture in response to the deep sense of gratitude she felt for his patience and love. Isaac paused, looking over at her with a gentle smile.

"You're looking better every day," he said, his thumb brushing lightly over her knuckles.

Mary smiled back, nodding. "I feel better, Isaac. It's hard to explain, but it's like…like I've been given a second chance."

Isaac squeezed her hand, his eyes shining with emotion.

A soft knock on the door interrupted the moment, and Hannah entered, carrying a tray with a bowl of warm soup and some freshly baked bread. She smiled warmly as she approached the bed and set the tray down on the small table beside Mary.

"Here we go," said Hannah, her voice full of gentle encouragement. "Some nice chicken soup and bread from the bakery. I thought you might be ready for something a little more substantial."

Hannah handed the bowl of soup to Mary,

who took it carefully, feeling its warmth seeping into her hands. The smell of the soup, rich and comforting, filled the room, and Mary suddenly realized how hungry she was. She hadn't felt such an appetite in weeks.

Mary's eyes softened with gratitude. "*Danki*, Hannah. You've been so kind, helping us like this."

Hannah waved off the thanks with a smile. "It's been a pleasure to help you, Mary."

Isaac stood up, giving Hannah a nod of appreciation. "I'm just going to pack up the rest of the *Grischtdaag* orders," he said. "I cannot believe *Grischtnacht* is already upon us."

Mary smiled at him as he turned to go, then took another careful sip of her soup. It felt good to eat something substantial and nourishing again, to feel her body regaining its strength bit by bit. As she set the spoon down, she looked up to see that Hannah had pulled up a chair next to her and was taking a seat.

Hannah smiled warmly—though Mary noticed a flicker of something in her eyes; was it uncertainty? Mary decided to ask about it.

"How are things going?" Mary asked gently. "Isaac told me about Daniel."

Hannah's smile faltered, and she looked down at her hands, fidgeting slightly. "*Ya*, well… things are progressing," she said softly, her tone lacking its usual cheerfulness.

Mary tilted her head and studied Hannah's expression. "But you don't seem very happy about it. Is something wrong?"

Hannah sighed, her shoulders slumping as she met Mary's concerned gaze. "Daniel is a *gut* friend, and my *vadder* likes him very much. He's steady and kind, and he would be a *gut mann*. But…" She hesitated, searching for the right words. "But I don't have those kinds of feelings for him, Mary."

Mary nodded slowly, understanding dawning. "And what about Levi?" she pressed softly, her eyes searching Hannah's face.

Hannah's eyes widened in surprise, and she blushed slightly, caught off guard by Mary's perceptiveness.

"Isaac and I have both noticed the way he looks at you—the spark between you two."

Hannah wavered, the color high in her cheeks. "Levi…" she began, her voice trailing off as she tried to gather her thoughts. "Levi is *wunderbaar*. He's kind, and he's been so helpful these past few days. But...things with him are complicated."

"Complicated, how?" Mary prompted gently, encouraging her to continue.

Hannah sighed, her gaze dipping to her hands again.

"Is this about Emma?" Mary asked astutely. "Isaac told me she came to see Levi."

Hannah nodded. "With Daniel, everything is safe and familiar. I know what to expect from him, and my *vadder* approves. And everyone in the *gmay* expects us to marry. Levi...he makes me feel things I've never felt for anyone before. My *daed* doesn't know him very well, but it's all a moot point because he's engaged to Emma. I thought he had feelings for me, but I must have misconstrued his kindness as more than just that; Emma was already his fiancée before he arrived here in Willowvale. Saying yes to Daniel just seemed like the next best thing to do. There's no one else I can see myself marrying in our *gmay*."

Mary listened attentively, and her heart went out to Hannah. She could see the turmoil her friend was experiencing, torn between what her heart truly wanted, the reality of Levi's engagement to Emma, and what was expected of her. After a moment, she reached out and took Hannah's hand, squeezing it gently.

"Hannah," Mary began, her voice soft but firm. "I understand that it's tempting to choose what feels safe and familiar, especially when there's pressure from those we love and by our circumstances. But marriage is a lifelong commitment. It's about more than just what makes sense pragmatically. It's about finding someone who brings light into your life, who makes life's experiences, both good and bad, better, who spurs you in your faith and directs you closer to *Gott,* and who stands by your side no matter what difficulties might occur."

Hannah regarded Mary, her eyes reflecting her uncertainty. "But how can I tell Levi how I feel when he's courting Emma? And what if I misinterpreted what I thought were signs of him having feelings for me? Making a mistake in that assumption would be a hundred times more embarrassing if his heart does, in fact, belong to Emma."

Mary smiled gently, seeing so much of her younger self in Hannah. "Love is always a risk," she said sagely. "There are no guarantees. But if you care for Levi, if you feel that spark of love with him, then it's worth exploring. Maybe he is engaged to Emma, but that was before he met you. Perhaps he even feels about Emma as you do about Daniel. It would be far less hurtful if he were to break things off with her now, especially if your feelings are requited, than to go ahead and marry her. You both deserve to be with someone who loves you deeply; you deserve someone who recognizes you for the person you are, despite your failings, and who wants to share his life with you."

Hannah bit her lip, considering Mary's words. "But Daniel...he's everything I should want in a *mann*. He's steady, and he'll be a *gut* provider. My *vadder* thinks highly of him, and I know I won't disappoint anyone if I choose him. Also, I agreed to be courted by him. It will complicate everything if I change my mind."

Mary squeezed her hand again. "But what do *you* want, Hannah? What is your heart telling you?"

Hannah looked down, her thoughts swirling. "My heart...my heart is confused. I care about Daniel, but I don't feel the same way about him as I do about Levi. With Levi, there's...there's something different. It's as if he sees me, really sees me, in a way no one else does. I feel an excitement, a breathlessness when I'm with him."

Mary nodded, her expression thoughtful. "Then maybe that's something worth paying attention to. You ought to be with someone who makes you feel special. And Levi is also a reliable, decent, hardworking *mann*. He is already respected in the *gmay*."

Hannah met Mary's gaze. Her eyes still reflected uncertainty but also held a tinge of hope and purpose. "Do you really think so, Mary?"

"I do," Mary replied with conviction. "And I think you owe it to yourself to consider what your heart truly wants and where you believe *Gott* is guiding you. Don't settle for what's safe just because everybody expects it. Choose the path that feels right to you, the one that will bring you the most happiness in the future. It might be a bit awkward for a while, but your *vadder* will accept it. He wants you to be happy. And it will be hard for Daniel, but it will be harder for him in the long run when he realizes you married him for the wrong reasons and feel little more than friendship for him. And he will realize in time."

Hannah nodded slowly, taking in Mary's words. "*Danki*, Mary. I...I'll think about what you've said."

Mary smiled warmly, giving Hannah's hand one final squeeze. "Take your time, Hannah. And whatever you decide, know that I'm here for you, no matter what."

Hannah's expression softened, and she leaned in to give Mary a gentle hug.

Mary looked up over Hannah's shoulder to see Isaac returning. He smiled at her, and his expression softened with relief when he saw the calm in her eyes.

Hannah stood, turned, and smoothed down her apron. "I should get back to the bakery," she said, glancing at the clock on the wall. "The *weiwer* are meeting soon to figure out where to continue their quilting circle for the time being now that the community center is temporarily unavailable."

Mary's thoughts raced. The quilting circle had always been a cherished part of her life since it provided a way to connect with the other women in the community. Too consumed by grief to participate, she had distanced herself from it after Grace's death. But now, the thought of being part of that circle again, of contributing in some way, filled her with a surprising sense of anticipation.

Before she could fully think it through, the words were out of her mouth. "They could meet here."

Hannah and Isaac turned to her in unison, surprise evident on their faces.

"Are you sure?" Hannah asked, eyes wide with astonishment.

Concern flickered in Isaac's eyes. "Are you feeling strong enough for that? It's a big step."

Mary nodded emphatically. "*Ya.* I've been absent from the *gmay* for too long. It's time for me to rejoin, to be part of something I value again. I want to help, and this is a way I can do that."

Hannah's surprise gave way to a warm, encouraging smile. "That's *wunderbaar*, Mary. I think it would mean a lot to everyone to have the circle here."

Mary mirrored her smile, feeling a sense of purpose take root. "Please let the other *weiwer* know they're *willkumm* to *kumm* here. It would be lovely to have them."

Hannah nodded. "I will. They'll be so happy to hear it. And I'll be here to cater for the circle. All the other *weiwer* will help as well."

Isaac watched Mary closely, his expression one of both pride and cautious optimism. He reached out and took her hand with a firm but gentle grip. "If you're sure, Mary, then I support you."

Mary squeezed his hand, feeling the warmth of his support. "I'm sure, Isaac. I need this."

Hannah gathered her things, still smiling as she prepared to leave. "I'll let everyone know."

As Hannah left, Mary felt a stirring of anticipation and excitement at the thought of seeing her friends from the community again. Opening her home to the quilting circle was more than just a gesture; it was a step toward reclaiming her life, toward reconnecting with the community that had been there for her since she was born into it.

Isaac turned to her with eyes filled with admiration. "You're amazing, you know that?"

Mary chuckled softly. "I'm just trying to find my way back, Isaac. I'm tired of living in the shadows."

Isaac leaned in and kissed her forehead. "I'm proud of you."

∞∞∞

That afternoon, as the sun dipped lower in the sky, casting a soft golden light across the room, Mary prepared for the community quilting circle, the idea of having the women gather in her home both exciting and frightening. It had been so long since she participated in anything social, and she was worried about how she would feel once everyone arrived. But she knew it was time to take the step, to rejoin the world she had not been able to face for so long.

As was the current norm, Isaac was by her side. He helped her get dressed since her limbs still felt weak and the simple act of putting on a dress took more energy than she anticipated. But Isaac was patient and his touch gentle as he guided her arms through the sleeves and fastened the buttons.

"Are you sure you're ready for this?" Isaac asked, concern evident in his voice as he helped her to her feet.

Mary looked at him and nodded. "I am," she asserted.

With Isaac's support, she made her way to the sitting room. The space had been transformed into a welcoming haven for the quilting circle, with chairs arranged in a ring and the warm scent of freshly brewed tea filling the air.

As they settled her into a comfortable chair, Mary took a deep breath, trying to calm the fluttering in her chest. Isaac placed a gentle hand on her shoulder, giving her a reassuring squeeze before stepping back; she was ready to greet the guests.

The first knock at the door was quickly followed by others, and soon, the room was filled with the familiar faces of the women from the community. Each one greeted Mary with warmth and genuine happiness at seeing her out of bed and sitting among them. There were hugs, hand squeezes, and words of encouragement that made Mary's heart swell with gratitude.

"*Ach*, Mary," said Ruth Yoder, a sturdy woman with a heart-shaped face and kind eyes. She enveloped Mary in a warm hug. "It's *gut* to see you up and about. We've missed you so much."

"We've all been praying for you," added Eliza Bontrager, her voice gentle as she sat down next to Mary. "You've been in our thoughts every day."

"*Danki*," Mary replied softly, her voice thick with emotion. "It means the world to me to have you all here."

The women settled into their seats, and each one pulled out her current quilting project. The rhythmic sound of needles being pressed through fabric soon filled the room, accompanied by the soft hum of conversation. Mary picked up her own quilting square, her hands trembling slightly as she threaded the needle. The task was familiar, but it felt strange after so much time. Her hands had been idle since Grace died.

At first, Mary felt awkward and out of place, as if she were intruding on a world that had moved on without her. The women, discerning her unease, offered gentle support without pressing her to talk. They shared stories and memories, filling the room with warmth and laughter.

"Do you remember the time Ruth tried to teach us how to make apple butter and ended up burning the entire batch?" Esther Troyer chirped, her eyes twinkling with mischief.

Ruth chuckled, shaking her head. "It wasn't that bad!"

"It was worse!" exclaimed Eliza, laughing. "The kitchen smelled like burnt sugar for days!"

The room erupted in laughter, and Mary found herself smiling as the tension in her shoulders eased. The women continued to share funny anecdotes, and their voices soothed Mary's fragile spirit.

"Do you remember when we tried to surprise the bishop with a quilt for his birthday and he ended up walking in on us before it was finished?" Emma Lehman added, her eyes dancing with mirth.

"*Ach*, he pretended he didn't see a thing," Ruth added, her shoulders shaking with laughter. "But he couldn't hide his smile. I'm pretty sure he knew exactly what we were up to."

As the stories flowed, Mary felt herself relaxing into the rhythm of the conversation and the steady motion of her hands stitching the quilt. The awkwardness gradually faded and was replaced by a sense of belonging she hadn't felt in months. The quilting circle quickly became a sanctuary, a place where she could find comfort in the collective warmth of the women around her.

Eliza leaned over and gently patted Mary's hand. "It really is so *gut* to see you smile, Mary. You've been through so much, but you're strong. Stronger than you know."

Mary's eyes welled with tears, but this time, they were tears of gratitude. "*Danki*, Eliza. I didn't realize how much I missed this...missed all of you."

"We've missed you, too, Mary and we're here for you," Ruth declared firmly. "Always."

As the afternoon wore on, with the room filled with the comforting sounds of the women's voices, laughter, and the soft rustling of fabric, Mary felt a lightness in her heart and a sense of healing that she hadn't thought possible. The grief was still there, but it no longer felt crushing and unbearable. It was something she could carry with the help of those around her, living out the Biblical mandate to bear one another's burdens in community.

At one point, she looked up and caught Isaac's eye as he stood in the doorway, watching the scene unfold. His eyes were filled with pride and tenderness, and when she smiled at him, she saw how his shoulders relaxed as the tension he had been carrying for so long finally eased.

Mary felt more like herself than she had in months; she knew that she was exactly where she needed to be—surrounded by love, quilting and sharing stories with dear companions, and healing in the warmth of friendship—slowly but surely reclaiming her life.

Chapter Twelve

Hannah stood in the bakery wiping down the counters and making sure everything was in order before closing up for the night. Outside, the sky was darkening, and a light snow had begun to fall, adding a soft hush to the evening.

As she worked, Hannah's thoughts drifted to Levi. He had been leading the rebuilding efforts at the community center, and despite how much she wanted to see him, their paths hadn't crossed since the fire.

Just as she was about to turn off the lights, the bell above the door chimed, and she looked up to see Levi stepping into the bakery. His coat was dusted with snow, and he looked tired but determined, his eyes locking onto hers as he entered.

"Levi," Hannah breathed softly, surprised and pleased to see him. "I didn't expect you."

Levi smiled with a warmth in his eyes that set Hannah's heart rate into overdrive. "I wanted to see you, Hannah. We haven't had a chance to talk."

Hannah nodded, her stomach fluttering with anticipation and nervousness. "I'm glad you came, but...Daniel will be here soon to walk me home."

Levi's expression faltered, but then he took a step closer to her, closing the distance between them. "Hannah, I have to ask you...do you really want to be with Daniel?"

Hannah hesitated, aware that her heart was pounding in her chest. She had been wrestling with that very question, unsure of how to navigate the feelings swirling inside her. "It's complicated. My *vadder* approves of Daniel, and he's been a *gut* friend. But..."

"But what?" Levi pressed gently, his voice soft but insistent.

Hannah looked down as her hands fidgeted with the edge of her apron. "But I don't feel the way I should. I don't have strong feelings for him, not in the way I think I should if we're going to get married. And I've been so confused because... well, because of you."

Levi's eyes softened, and he reached out to gently lift her chin so she would meet his gaze. "Hannah," he said, his eyes searching hers.

But Hannah took a step back, shaking her head.

"What is it?" he asked.

"Emma. She told me she's your fiancée; she came to Willowvale for you."

"She was referring to the past and speaking what she was hoping in her heart. She did *kumm* here for me," he confessed. "But not because we are still engaged; she was hoping to give things another go. Before I came here tonight, I went to see her and told her to go back home."

Hannah's heart lifted at his words, hope blooming inside her like a rose unfurling in the warm sunlight. "You...you did?"

Levi nodded, his eyes never leaving hers. "*Ya.* Emma is a *wunderbaar* person, but my heart isn't with her anymore. It's with you, Hannah. I've felt something between us from the moment we met, and I can't ignore it. I don't want to."

Tears prickled at the corners of Hannah's

eyes. She hadn't expected, hadn't dared to hope that Levi felt the same way she did. "Levi, I…I feel the same. I've tried to deny it, but I can't. There's something between us, something tangible."

Levi grinned, relief and happiness flooding his face. "I'm so glad you feel the same."

Hannah nodded, then disclosed, "My *vadder*…he wants me to marry Daniel. He thinks Daniel is the best choice for me, and I don't want to hurt Daniel, either. He's been nothing but kind to me."

Levi took her hands in his; his touch was warm and reassuring. "I can't tell you what to do, but I can tell you that if you don't feel happy with Daniel, then you owe it to yourself and to him to be honest—before it's too late and you end up in a miserable marriage."

Hannah looked into Levi's eyes, seeing the sincerity and love there. "I'm afraid," she confessed.

"I'm afraid, too," Levi admitted, his voice low. "But whatever happens, I'll be here for you."

A surge of emotion washed over Hannah, and before she could think before acting, she leaned in and pressed her lips to Levi's in a soft, tentative kiss that was filled with all the feelings she had been holding back. Levi responded gently, his hand moving to cup her cheek as he deepened the kiss.

When they finally pulled away, both of them were breathless, and Hannah's heart was racing. But before either could say anything, the bell above the door jangled again, and they both turned to see Daniel standing there. Levi stepped back, releasing her hand, and Hannah felt a wave of guilt wash over her, feeling like the proverbial child caught with their hand in the cookie jar.

"Hannah, are you ready to go?" Daniel asked, his voice tight.

Levi glanced at Hannah, his eyes shining with understanding. "I should go," he said quietly, stepping toward the door.

Hannah's heart sank as she watched Levi leave, and the door closed softly behind him. She turned to Daniel, feeling the storm of emotions still swirling inside her. She knew she needed to face things, to be honest with Daniel about her feelings, but the words stuck in her throat.

As they left the bakery together, Hannah silently prayed for a Christmas miracle, for the strength to follow her heart and make the right choices, even if it meant difficult conversations and facing the disappointment of those she loved.

∞ ∞ ∞

Hannah walked beside Daniel, her mind racing as they made their way through the quiet snow-coated streets. The world around her seemed to blur as Daniel spoke in a steady stream of words about the future, about their life together once they were married. But Hannah found it hard to focus since her heart was in her throat as she replayed her conversation with Levi over and over in her mind.

"I was thinking," Daniel continued, "that after we're married, we could start planning to build our own place on my *familye's* land. It's close enough to the village but with enough space for a nice garden and maybe even a few animals. What do you think?"

Hannah nodded absently, her thoughts distant. She could barely register the plans Daniel was so eagerly laying out before her. All she could think about was how wrong it felt, how the future he was describing wasn't the one she truly wanted.

"And we could get started on the house this spring," Daniel continued, his tone filled with the excitement of someone whose dreams were within reach. "I've already spoken to my *vadder* about it, and he's more than willing to help with the costs. We'll have a cozy home, perfect for starting a *familye*."

The words "starting a *familye*" were like a bucket of cold water being thrown on Hannah's distracted state. How could she build a life with Daniel when her heart was elsewhere? She couldn't. Her heart twisted painfully, and a deep, gnawing sense of dread filled her.

As they approached her house, Hannah knew she couldn't go on pretending that everything was fine when it wasn't. She had to tell Daniel the truth, no matter how much it hurt him, no matter how much it might disappoint her father.

With her house just a few steps away, Hannah took a deep breath and turned to Daniel, her heart pounding. "Daniel, there's something I need to talk to you about..."

But before she could get the words out, the front door of her house opened and her father stepped out onto the porch, his expression warm and welcoming.

"Hannah, Daniel," Bishop Weaver called out, his voice filled with a fatherly affection that made Hannah's heart ache even more. "We've been waiting for you."

"We?" Hannah practically squeaked.

"Mr. and Mrs. King are here for dinner," her father replied. "Or have you forgotten?"

Hannah had forgotten.

"*Ach*, right," she said.

As they walked up the steps to the porch, Hannah forced a smile that didn't reach her eyes. Her father's approval meant a great deal to her, and she knew how pleased he would be if she married Daniel. But how could she go through with it when her heart was telling her something entirely different?

The dinner table was set with care. Bishop Weaver sat at the head, with Daniel on his right and Hannah on his left. Mr. and Mrs. King were seated opposite each other, their smiles warm and welcoming. Mrs. King had prepared a casserole, a dish for which she was well known, and it steamed from its place in the center of the table, deliciously fragrant.

Despite the homey and hospitable scene,

Hannah could hardly bring herself to eat. Her heart felt lodged in her stomach, which was churning with anxiety, leaving no room for food. She pushed the food around on her plate, trying to appear engaged in the conversation, but her mind was elsewhere—on Levi, Daniel, and the expectations of her father and the Kings.

Bishop Weaver, ever the gracious host, kept the conversation going. "The church rebuilding is coming along nicely," he said, his tone measured and approving. "I have to say, young Mr. Miller is doing a commendable job leading the effort. I was hesitant at first given that he's new to our *gmay*, but the *menner* seem to like him."

Mr. King nodded in agreement, turning his attention to Hannah. "So, Hannah, I understand Mr. Miller is a friend of yours? What's he like?"

The question caught Hannah off guard, especially since her thoughts at that moment were centered on Levi, and she felt her face flush with sudden heat. She stammered, and her words tumbled out awkwardly. "Levi? *Ach*, um, he's...he's kind and hardworking. Very dedicated to helping out...especially with the rebuild..."

She could feel Daniel's gaze on her, his

frown deepening as he witnessed her flustered response. The room seemed to close in around her with the ceiling and walls pressing in.

"Well, perhaps he will be available to help build your new house," Mr. King remarked. "Daniel has some grand ideas."

"I don't need his help," Daniel insisted.

Mr. King chuckled, sitting back in his chair. "Now, Daniel," he said. "You may be *gut* at many things, but Mr. Miller is a carpenter. You could use someone with a little experience."

Daniel's mouth pressed into a hard line.

"And how is Mrs. Fisher doing, Hannah?" Mrs. King asked, steering the conversation in another direction. "We've all been so worried about her."

"She's much better, *danki*," answered Hannah, ever so grateful for the change in topic. "She's getting stronger every day. It's been a blessing to witness her recovery."

"Hannah has been at Mary's bedside almost every day," Daniel said, smiling. "She has the kindest heart."

Hannah blushed, unable to meet his eye.

A brief hush fell over the table.

Unexpectedly, Daniel reached for Hannah's

hand, and she stiffened, her heart hammering as she looked up to meet his gaze. His smile was warm and full of hope.

"Hannah," Daniel began. "I have something important to tell you."

Hannah's stomach twisted with dread. "What is it?" she asked, trying to keep her voice steady.

Daniel smiled and glanced around the table at the others present. "Since we've known each other our entire lives, our *eldre* have suggested that we marry after *Grischtdaag*. There's no reason to delay."

Hannah's world seemed to tilt on its axis, the words shaking her to the core. "What?" she whispered, her voice barely audible.

"Daniel is a fine young man, Hannah," her father asserted. "We believe this is the right path for both of you."

Mr. and Mrs. King nodded approvingly.

"I'm sure you two are excited to begin your lives together," Mrs. King said animatedly. "Hannah has always been like a *dochder* to us, and now it will be official. We will all be *familye*."

"Isn't it *wunderbaar*?" Daniel gushed, his eyes bright with anticipation.

But it wasn't wonderful for Hannah. Coils of constrictions crushed her chest, almost suffocating her. The future that Daniel and her father were planning for her felt like a cage, one from which she couldn't escape.

"I..." Hannah stammered, her heart pounding in her ears. "I need to be excused."

She pushed her chair back so abruptly that it tipped over, crashing to the floor. Her bewildering behavior and alarming clamor startled everyone, but Hannah was oblivious in her distress. She rushed from the room, her vision blurring with tears.

As she fled the dining room, the sounds of everyone calling after her receded into the background. She needed air, she needed space, she needed to think. Her heart felt as if it were being rent in two, and she had no idea what to do next. All she knew was that she couldn't marry Daniel.

"Hannah?"

She turned to see her father standing in the doorway.

"*Vadder*," Hannah said, holding her heaving chest.

"What is the matter? Are you ill?"

Hannah swallowed thickly, unable to meet her father's gaze. She was so conflicted, torn between the expectations placed on her, especially by her well-meaning father, and the truth buried deep in her heart. "I...I just needed some air," she whispered, her voice trembling.

Her father sighed, his hand remaining on her shoulder as he looked out into the snowy night. "I know things are moving quickly, Hannah, but Daniel is a *gut mann*. You've known each other since you were *kinner*. He will treat you well and provide for you. That's all I have ever wanted for you."

Hannah's stomach clenched. She knew her father genuinely believed this was the best path for her. But he was wrong.

Bishop Weaver continued in a gentle but firm tone. "I'm proud of you, Hannah. You've grown into a fine *fraa*, and I know your *maem* would be proud, too. She always wanted to see you settled with a *familye* of your own."

The mention of her mother made Hannah's throat tighten with emotion. Her mother's absence was a constant ache in her heart, and she strived to live up to the woman her mother had been. But now, with this decision looming over her, she felt more lost than ever.

"I want to see you happy, Hannah," her father continued. "I want to see you start your own *familye*, to have the kind of love and stability that your mother and I had. Daniel can give you that."

Hannah's emotions swirled in a ferocious storm; she wanted to tell her father everything, to pour out her heart and explain that she couldn't marry Daniel because she didn't feel for him the way a woman should feel for the man who was to be her husband. But the words wouldn't come. She felt trapped, unable to voice her true feelings, afraid of disappointing the man who had always been there for her.

Bishop Weaver gently squeezed her shoulder, his gaze warm and reassuring. "*Kumm* back inside, Hannah. It's cold out here, and everyone's worried about you."

Hannah nodded numbly, her throat too tight to speak. She followed her father back inside, her legs leaden. When they returned to the dining room, the warmth of the house did little to chase away the chill in her bones.

As she took her seat at the table, Daniel looked at her with an expression of concern. "Are you okay?"

Hannah forced a smile though it felt brittle on her lips. "I...I just needed some air."

Daniel smiled, relieved, and reached for her hand under the table. His touch, intended to be warm and comforting, only made the knots in her stomach intensify.

The conversation at the table resumed with talk of their future together, plans for the house they would build, the family they would start. Everyone seemed so certain, so pleased with the way things were falling into place. All Hannah could do was nod and smile; the words on the tip of her tongue never made it past her lips.

She felt like an observer in her own life, watching as decisions were made for her and as her future was laid out before her, detail by detail, without her consent. The more they talked, the more isolated and trapped she felt, her heart screaming for something different, something true.

∞∞∞

Christmas morning dawned crisp and clear, with the world outside Hannah's window blanketed in a fresh layer of snow that sparkled in the early light. Inside, the house was quiet, the comforting warmth of the fire her father had already lit in the hearth spreading heat to ward off the chill.

Hannah dressed slowly, her mind still heavy with the events of the previous evening. She had barely slept. Her thoughts raced as she replayed the conversation with her father and the plans for her future that were unfolding without her true consent. But she knew she had to push those thoughts aside for the time being. It was Christmas, after all.

She made her way downstairs, and the aroma of breakfast was already wafting through the house. Her father was in the kitchen, humming a quiet tune as he prepared their usual Christmas breakfast—pancakes, eggs, and thick slices of ham. It was a simple meal, but it was a tradition they kept since her mother passed, a small way of honoring the woman who had always made Christmas special.

"*Frehlicher Grischtdaag, Vadder,*" Hannah greeted softly as she entered the kitchen, offering her father a small smile.

"*Frehlicher Grischtdaag,* Hannah."

They ate breakfast together in the cozy kitchen, the only sounds being the crackling of the fire and the occasional clink of cutlery on plates. The quiet of the morning was soothing, and Hannah tried to focus on the present, on the simple joy of sharing the occasion with her father.

After breakfast, they retreated to the sitting room, where the small tree stood, decorated with handmade ornaments, and whose branches harbored a couple of presents at its base. The tree was simple yet brought warmth and light to the room, reminding Hannah of all the Christmases they had spent together, first with her mother and then just the two of them.

"Why don't you open yours first?" Bishop Weaver suggested.

Hannah smiled and reached for the package, carefully unwrapping it to reveal a beautifully carved wooden box. She recognized her father's handiwork immediately. The intricate patterns and careful craftsmanship were a testament to the love and care he had put into making it.

"*Ach*, *Vadder*, it's beautiful," she whispered in awe, running her fingers over the smooth wood.

"It's for your quilting supplies," her father

explained. "I thought it might be nice to have something special to keep them in."

"*Danki*. I'll cherish it always."

Hannah reached for her father's gift and handed it to him.

"This is for you," she said.

Bishop Weaver took the gift from her. "What's this, now?" he asked as he carefully unwrapped the paper.

When he finally uncovered the gift, he smiled. "New gloves," he said, pleased, holding them up to admire the craftsmanship. The leather was soft and sturdy, clearly made to last.

"I noticed your old ones were looking rather worn," Hannah explained. "I thought you could use a new pair."

Her father slipped the gloves on, flexing his fingers to test the fit. "*Danki*, Hannah."

Hannah's smile grew. "I'm glad you like them. I wanted to get you something you could actually use."

After they exchanged gifts, her father retired to his study, leaving Hannah alone. She cleaned up the kitchen with her stomach still in knots. She wanted to talk to her father, to tell him what was truly in her heart, but every time she tried to find the words and the courage, the fear of disappointing him held her back. She knew how much her father wanted to see her settled and starting a family of her own, and she didn't want to take that away from him. But at the same time, she couldn't ignore the truth—her heart was pulling her in a different direction, one that didn't include Daniel.

Hannah left the kitchen, walked to the study, and knocked on the door.

"*Kumm* in," answered Bishop Weaver.

She cautiously opened the door. "*Vadder*," she began hesitantly, her voice quiet.

"What is it, Hannah?" he asked, not looking up from the open book on the desk in front of him.

Hannah vacillated, her throat tightening with the emotions she was struggling to hold back. "I just...I want you to know how much I appreciate everything you've done for me—"

A knock at the front door interrupted her, and her father looked up.

"Would you see who it is, please?" he asked.

Hannah nodded as she turned and walked down the hallway to the front door. She opened the door to find Daniel standing there with a warm smile on his face and his cheeks pink from the cold.

"*Frehlicher Grischtdaag*, Hannah," he greeted, his voice full of cheer.

"*Frehlicher Grischtdaag*, Daniel," Hannah reciprocated, forcing a smile.

The knots of anxiety in her stomach twisted and tightened as she saw him looking so hopeful and kind.

"I was wondering," Daniel continued, "if I might escort you to the sing-along at the Yoders' barn. I thought it would be nice to go together."

Hannah paused as her mind raced. But before she could find a valid excuse, her father appeared behind her.

"You should go, Hannah," Bishop Weaver encouraged.

"Are you sure, *Vadder*? You don't mind being left alone today?"

"*Ya*, I'll be fine. I could use the time to prepare my next sermon."

Hannah looked up at her father, whose eyes were resolute.

"All right," she finally agreed.

She grabbed her shawl and *kapp* before stepping outside with Daniel. He led her to the buggy, helping her up into the seat before climbing in beside her. As they set off, the rhythmic clip-clop of the horse's hooves on the snow-sprinkled road filled the silence between them.

Daniel chatted away, his tone light and filled with excitement about the gathering. Hannah listened, but her responses were automatic since her mind wasf still preoccupied with the conflict in her heart.

The snowy landscape and the peace of the morning contrasted sharply with the turmoil Hannah felt inside. She wished she could feel the same sense of ease that Daniel seemed to have, but every word he spoke only reminded her of the decisions she had yet to make.

When they finally arrived at the Yoder barn, the soft light of lanterns spilling out from the open doors welcomed them. The barn was beautifully decorated with garlands of evergreen, and the faint sounds of the people already gathering inside could be heard, their voices merry with holiday cheer.

Before Hannah could climb down from the buggy, Daniel touched her arm gently. "Wait just a sec," he said.

He reached into his coat pocket, his expression both excited and nervous. "I have something for you," he said, pulling out a small wrapped package. He held it out to her. *"Frehlicher Grischtdaag."*

Hannah stared at the gift in his hand, her confusing emotions a muddled tangled mess. Slowly, she reached out and accepted the package from him. Her fingers trembled slightly as she unwrapped it.

Inside, was a delicate white handkerchief.

"It's lovely. *Danki*, Daniel."

He smiled, relief evident in his expression. "I'm glad you like it."

Daniel reached for her hand, squeezing it gently. "I just wanted to give you something special, something that shows how much you mean to me."

Hannah forced a smile though it felt hollow.

He nodded, seeming satisfied with her response, then helped her down from the buggy. They walked toward the barn together.

As Hannah and Daniel stepped into the warmth of the Yoder barn, Hannah was momentarily overwhelmed by the bustle of the gathering. The barn was filled with familiar faces, all shining with the warmth of Christmas cheer, and the smell of pine and fresh hay mingled with the scent of hot cider as the soft hum of conversation and laughter created a comforting vibe.

Hannah instinctively scanned the crowd and quickly spotted Levi. He stood near the rear of the barn, surrounded by Rachel, Conrad, Anna, and Eli. They were talking and laughing, and the children were tugging playfully at Levi's coat as he tried to keep them in line. When he caught sight of Hannah, his expression softened, and a warm smile formed on his lips.

Their eyes met across the barn, the connection between them magnetic and undeniable. But just as quickly, Hannah looked away, her heart racing. The warmth of Levi's gaze lingered in her awareness even after she turned her attention back to the crowd, but she couldn't let herself dwell on it. Not there, not then.

A familiar voice afforded her a welcome distraction.

She turned to see Mary and Isaac making their way toward her. Her face lit up at the sight of them, and she hurried forward eagerly.

"Mary, Isaac! It's so *gut* to see you both."

Mary, looking more energetic and healthier than Hannah had seen her in weeks, smiled. The noticeable lightness in her step and the renewed strength in her manner caused Hannah's heart to swell with happiness and gratefulness.

"Hannah, I'm so pleased to see you," Mary said warmly, reaching out to hug her.

Hannah returned the hug, feeling a deep sense of relief and joy at seeing Mary looking so well. "*Frehlicher Grischtdaag*, Mary. You look *wunderbaar*. I'm so glad to see you out and about."

Isaac smiled beside her, his expression one of quiet pride as he watched his wife and Hannah. "Mary's been getting stronger every day. We're grateful for the prayers and support from everyone, especially you, Hannah."

Mary reached into the small bag she was carrying and pulled out a package wrapped in brown paper. "I have something for you," she said, her voice tender.

Hannah blinked in surprise as she accepted the package, glancing up at Mary in confusion. "For me? What is it?"

"Open it," Mary encouraged with a gentle smile.

Hannah carefully unwrapped the package. When she finally pulled back the paper, her breath caught in her throat. Inside was Grace's quilt, the one Mary had made with so much love and care, the one that was wrapped around Grace in her final days.

Hannah's eyes brimmed with tears as she looked up at Mary, overwhelmed by the gift. "Mary...I...I can't accept this. It's too precious."

Mary's smile was soft but insistent. "We want you to have it, Hannah. For your *kinner*, when the time comes."

Hannah blinked rapidly, trying to keep the tears at bay, but it was to no avail. "I don't know what to say...*Danki*, Mary. To you both."

Isaac, who had been watching the exchange with a warm smile, gently patted Hannah on the shoulder. "*Nee* more tears now," he admonished in a paternal tone.

Hannah nodded, swallowing the lump in her throat as she carefully folded the quilt and hugged it against her chest. "I'll cherish it always," she whispered, her voice thick with emotion.

Mary smiled, her eyes warm with kindness and understanding. "It's a piece of Grace, a piece of our *familye*, and now it's with you."

Mr. Yoder stepped up to the front of the barn, raising his hands to call for attention. The conversations and laughter slowly petered out as everyone turned their focus to him, their faces reflecting the quiet joy of the Christmas season.

"Friends and *familye*," Mr. Yoder began, his voice carrying easily over the crowd. "It's time to begin our *Grischtdaag* sing-along. Let's raise our voices together in celebration of this blessed day."

There was a murmur of agreement, and people began to move into place, forming a loose circle around the inside perimeter of the barn. Hannah ended up standing between Daniel and Mary, with Isaac on Mary's other side. The familiar faces of the community surrounded them, and the warmth of their presence was akin to a comforting blanket on a cold winter's night.

Hannah pressed the quilt to her chest. Its warmth and weight provided a measure of comfort against the storm of emotions inside her. She glanced at Mary, who gave her a supportive smile, the kind that gave Hannah reassurance that everything would work out.

The first notes of "Silent Night" filled the

air, the soft, gentle melody drawing everyone in. Hannah joined in with the singing, her voice blending with those around her. It was a moment of peace, a shared connection that reminded her of the strength of the community, of the love that bound them all together.

As the words of the carol rose and fell, Hannah's gaze drifted across the circle, and she found herself looking for Levi. When she finally spotted him, her heart skipped a beat. He was standing with his sister, Rachel, and her family, his face serene as he sang. But then his eyes met hers, and for a few seconds, the world seemed to zoom in on just the two of them.

Something in Levi's gaze—something deep and unspoken—made Hannah's heart ache with longing. She could feel the connection between them, the pull that had been there since the first time they met. It was a feeling she couldn't ignore, no matter how hard she tried.

But her thoughts were interrupted by the warm pressure of Daniel's hand slipping into hers. Hannah's breath caught as she felt the solid, familiar grip of his hand, a gesture filled with affection and expectation. It was a gesture that should have made her feel secure, but instead, it only deepened her sense of confusion.

She glanced up at Daniel, who was singing with a smile on his face, completely unaware of the turmoil inside her. His hand was steady and warm, offering the kind of stability and certainty for which she knew she should be grateful. Yet, as much as she cared for Daniel, the depth of feeling she had for Levi was impossible to ignore.

The community continued to sing with the beautiful harmony of their voices rising to the barn rafters. Hannah tried to focus on the lyrics, attempting to find comfort in the familiar carols that had always brought her peace. But her heart was divided, torn between the path that had been laid out for her and the one she desperately wanted to follow.

As the final notes of "Silent Night" faded into the air, Hannah found herself standing at a crossroads. Daniel's fingers were still entwined with hers, a symbol of the life that awaited her if she chose to go down that path. But when she looked across the barn, Levi represented another choice—one filled with uncertainty but also with the possibility of a love that was genuine and true.

Hannah's eyes met Levi's once more, and

she knew that whatever happened next, she had to be honest with herself, with Daniel, and with everyone around her. The time for difficult conversations was imminent; she knew she couldn't put it off any longer.

As the community began the next carol, Hannah's voice joined in, but her heart was no longer in it. Instead, it was filled with the knowledge that Christmas, a time of peace and joy, had also become a time for her to face the truth and find the courage to follow her heart, wherever it might lead.

Chapter Thirteen

Isaac and Mary sat together with their fingers interlaced; the simple act of holding hands was a testament to the fractured bond that had begun to heal. He glanced at her, noting the peace in her expression and the way her eyes shone with a quiet joy that had been missing for so long. It filled him with gratitude—gratitude for her recovery, for her presence by his side, and for the love that, despite the hardships, had not been destroyed.

The room was filled with a gentle light. The crispness of the winter air occasionally drifted in through the gaps in the wooden walls. It was Christmas, a time of togetherness and reflection, and the barn seemed to cradle everyone in its embrace.

As they sang, the barn was alive with the sound of the community singing, voices blended in harmony as they offered up hymns and prayers. Each note seemed to rise to the rafters, a fragrant offering to God, a blessing to the souls of those present, and a reminder of the strength they found in their faith and in one another. Isaac's voice joined those of the others, but his mind was consumed by thoughts from which the singing failed to distract.

As he looked around the barn, his eyes fell on Hannah standing with Daniel by her side. But it wasn't Daniel who drew Isaac's attention—it was the way Hannah kept glancing across the barn, her eyes seeking out Levi, who stood with his sister's family. It was subtle, but Isaac saw it: the longing in her gaze, the way her eyes lit up a fraction when she found him in the crowd.

Isaac knew that look. He had seen it in Mary's eyes when they were younger, when their love was still new and fragile and the world seemed full of possibilities. It was a look that spoke of a heart yearning for something more, for a connection that was deep and true.

As the community continued to sing, Isaac felt a deep sense of empathy for the young couple. He knew the struggles they faced— Hannah with the expectations placed on her and Levi as the newcomer, finding his place in a community that could be slow to embrace change. Isaac understood the weight of those challenges, the way they could pull at the heart and cloud the mind.

Silently, Isaac bowed his head and offered a prayer. He prayed that God would guide Hannah and Levi and help them to navigate the challenges that lay before them while finding the strength to follow their hearts. He prayed that they would have the courage to be true to themselves, even when the path was difficult, and that they would find the love and happiness they both deserved.

Isaac felt a quiet resolve settle over him. He knew that God's hand was in everything and that the struggles and the joys were all part of a greater plan. He prayed that this plan would bring peace to Hannah's heart and that she would find the clarity she needed and that Levi would find his place in their community.

Beside him, Mary squeezed his hand gently, drawing him back to the present. He looked over at her, and she smiled, her eyes filled with understanding. She had seen the same thing as him and shared his concern and hope for the young couple.

"They'll find their way," Mary whispered, her voice soft but sure.

Isaac nodded, his heart filled with the same hope. "I believe they will."

Mary smiled at him tenderly, and Isaac's heart swelled. That Christmas, more than any other, felt like a new beginning—a chance to heal, to grow, and to move forward together.

As the final notes of the last hymn faded into the warm, hay-scented air of the barn, the gathered community slowly began to disperse. Isaac and Mary lingered a little, exchanging goodbyes and warm wishes with their friends and neighbors. The barn, now quieter, was still alight with the flicker of lanterns and the gentle hum of conversation. The warmth of the Christmas spirit lingered in every corner.

Isaac turned to Mary, her hand still comfortably resting in his, and smiled. "Shall we head home?" he asked softly.

Mary nodded, a contented smile on her lips. "*Ya.*"

They stepped out of the barn together into

the crisp, cold night. The air was fresh and sharp, carrying the faint scent of wood smoke from the nearby houses. Snow had begun to fall again, soft and silent, each flake catching the light of the lanterns and the moon above, creating an enchanted, sparkling blanket over the ground.

Isaac and Mary walked along the familiar path. The world around them was hushed, as the usual sounds of the village were muted by the thick layer of snow. The only sounds were the distant echo of laughter from the barn, the gentle rustling of the bare trees as the wind whispered through them, and the steady rhythm of their footsteps.

The path home wound through the heart of the village, past the small houses with their warm, glowing windows and smoke curling from the chimneys. The houses they passed bore signs of Christmas—wreaths fashioned from pine branches and holly, candles flickering in windows, and the occasional sound of carols drifting out from within.

As they walked, Mary leaned into Isaac, and he wrapped his arm around her, drawing her closer. The warmth of her presence beside him filled him with a deep sense of contentment, a feeling he had feared might be lost forever.

Before long, they reached their home. Inside, they shed their coats and boots, hanging them by the door. The house was cozy, filled with the quiet crackling of the fire Isaac had lit earlier, and its warmth spread through the rooms. They moved into the kitchen together. They had an unspoken agreement to prepare dinner as a team, something they had not done in a long time.

First, they set to work gathering ingredients for their Christmas meal, each item a cherished part of their holiday tradition. The kitchen was soon filled with the rich, familiar scents of the season, promising a feast that would warm both body and soul.

As Mary placed the large pot of chicken corn soup on the stove to simmer, Isaac got to work on the mashed potatoes that he had carefully peeled and boiled earlier that day. He added a generous amount of butter and a splash of fresh cream, mashing them to perfection: light and fluffy.

Then they turned their attention to the ham, the centerpiece of their Christmas meal. It was perfectly roasted, glazed with brown sugar, mustard, and a touch of honey—cooked slowly until the outside was caramelized and the meat tender and juicy.

"It looks *appeditlich*, Mary," complimented Isaac.

The sounds of their preparation—the soft clatter of dishes, the quiet hum of conversation, the sizzle of butter in the pan as Mary prepared some fresh greens—were comforting. The rich, savory scent of the meal mingled with the warmth of the fire.

Mary and Isaac also prepared a side dish of sweet and sour red cabbage, its vibrant color adding a festive touch to the table. The cabbage was slow-cooked with vinegar, sugar, and a hint of spices including ginger, cinnamon, and cloves, creating a dish that balanced tangy and sweet flavors perfectly.

The freshly baked bread, warm from the oven, its crust perfectly browned and the inside soft and fluffy, was accompanied by freshly churned creamy butter and a selection of preserves made from the summer's harvest —strawberry jam, apple butter, and peach preserves.

To round out the meal, there were pickled beets, their deep red color contrasting beautifully with the other dishes.

Just as they finished setting the table, there was a knock at the door followed by the familiar sound of Isaac's parents' voices. Isaac grinned, exchanging a quick glance with Mary before heading to the door to let them in.

"*Maem, Daed*," Isaac greeted warmly, opening the door to his parents, their faces flushed from the cold but beaming with happiness.

"*Frehlicher Grischtdaag*!" Ruth exclaimed as she stepped inside, shaking off the snow from her coat. "It's so *gut* to see you both."

"*Frehlicher Grischtdaag*!" Timothy echoed, clapping Isaac on the back with a hearty laugh. "I hope we're not too late for dinner!"

"Not at all," Mary replied, smiling as she came over to embrace them both. "We just finished getting everything ready. *Kumm*, sit and warm up."

The house quickly filled with the sounds of laughter and conversation, and the air was thick with the smell of good food and the warmth of family. The small kitchen seemed to expand, accommodating the joy that filled it. They all sat around the table, the meal before them transformed by the company and the spirit of the season.

Isaac couldn't help but think back to the last time they were all gathered around the table, when uncertainty and fear had weighed so heavily on his heart. It had been a dark time, one filled with worry for Mary, for their future, and for the life they worked so hard to build together. But that night felt different. The uncertainty had given way to hope, and the fear had been replaced by the quiet strength that came from enduring hardship together with God's empowerment and their community's support.

As they all bowed their heads to give thanks, Isaac silently added his own prayer of gratitude —for Mary's recovery, for the love they shared, and for the peace that had finally returned to their home. And as the evening wore on, filled with the sounds of stories, laughter, and the joy of simply being together, Isaac's heart swelled with a contentment that he knew he would carry with him long after the last candle had been blown out and the house had settled into quiet once more.

After a warm and joyful evening, Isaac's parents finally bundled themselves up and said their goodbyes, leaving behind the soft echoes of laughter and conversation that had filled their hearts. The kitchen, lively with the preparations and enjoyment of their Christmas meal only hours earlier, was now quiet save for the gentle clinking of dishes as Isaac and Mary tidied up.

Isaac glanced over at Mary as she placed the last of the dishes in the sink. Her movements were slow and deliberate, but there was a peace in her expression that hadn't been there for some time. He couldn't help but smile at the sight of her—his Mary, who had made it through so much, standing strong beside him.

"You must be tired," Isaac said gently, stepping over to her and placing a hand on her shoulder. "Why don't you go rest? I can finish cleaning up here."

Mary shook her head softly, turning to face him with a determined look in her eyes. "There's something else I want to do first."

His brow furrowed slightly as he sensed the gravity in her tone.

Mary reached out and took his hand, leading him away from the kitchen and down the hallway. Isaac followed without question, but his heart beat a little faster as he realized where she was leading him.

They stopped in front of Grace's room. The door, which had remained closed for so long, stood slightly ajar. Mary pushed it open, and the soft glow of the hallway light spilled into the small space, illuminating the room that had once been filled with the laughter and life of their little girl.

Neither of them said anything. Isaac's eyes roamed the room, taking in the small bed with its neatly folded quilt, the dollhouse in the corner, and the shelf lined with Grace's favorite books and toys. It was as if time had stood still in her room, preserving the memories of their daughter in every corner.

Mary finally broke the silence with her voice quiet but steady. "I want to pack away Grace's things. I want to give them to charity, to *kinner* who need them, so they may have something at *Grischtdaag*."

"Are you sure, Mary? It doesn't have to be now—"

But Mary shook her head firmly, her resolve clear. "*Ya*, Isaac. I want to do it now. It's time.

These things brought so much joy to Grace, and I want them to bring joy to other *kinner*. It's what she would have wanted."

Isaac looked into her eyes, reading the depth of her courage and love, and he knew she was ready. "All right," he agreed softly.

They moved quietly around the room, their actions filled with reverence and care. Mary started with the small clothes in the dresser, folding each piece carefully before placing it in a box. The little dresses and sweaters, the tiny socks and shoes—each item held memories, and Mary touched each one tenderly as if saying a silent goodbye.

Isaac's hands shook as he gathered Grace's wooden toys. He placed them gently in the box, remembering the way Grace's face had lit up when she played with them, her laughter echoing in his mind. The dollhouse, with its miniature furniture and tiny figures, went next. He closed his eyes, recalling the countless hours they had spent together, building little worlds and stories inside that house.

They worked together in silence, the only sounds coming from the soft rustling of fabric and the occasional creak of the floorboards. It was a solemn task, but there was a sense of peace that came with it—a release of the grief that had held them captive for so long.

When they had finished, the room felt different, emptier, but not in a way that was painful. Mary sat back down on the bed with her hands resting in her lap as she took one last look around the room. Isaac sat beside her and wrapped an arm around her shoulders.

"*Danki*, Isaac," Mary said softly, leaning into him "For helping me do this. It's hard, but…it feels right."

Isaac gently kissed the top of her head. His voice was thick with emotion. "We'll take these things to those who need them tomorrow. Grace's memory will live on in the smiles of other *kinner*."

Mary nodded, a tear slipping down her cheek, though this time, it was a tear of release, of acceptance. "*Ya*, Isaac. And I know she's smiling, too."

They sat for a little while longer, holding each other close, finding comfort in the shared task they had just completed. It was a step forward, a way of honoring Grace's memory while allowing themselves to heal, to move forward together.

When they finally stood up to leave the room, Isaac glanced back one last time at the empty bed and the now-clear shelves. It was no longer a place of sorrow but one of peace —a room where they had loved and been loved and where they could now let go, knowing that Grace's memory would always be with them.

As they left the room and closed the door gently behind them, Isaac squeezed Mary's hand, feeling a sense of deep connection and love. They were healing together.

Chapter Fourteen

L evi sat in his sister, Rachel's, cozy sitting room. The sound of crackling logs filled the space, mingling with the quiet giggles of Anna and Eli as they played on the carpet with their new wooden toys. The children were completely absorbed in their game, and the simple joy of Christmas lingered in their laughter.

Rachel watched them with a fond smile before gently interrupting. "All right, little ones, it's time for bed."

"Aww, do we have to?" Eli asked, his small hands still clutching his wooden horse.

"*Ya*, you do," Rachel replied, her tone kind but firm. "It's been a long, exciting day, and you need your rest."

Anna pouted, then obediently began to gather up the toys. "*Gude nacht, Onkel* Levi," she said, giving him a quick hug before heading toward the door.

"*Gude nacht, Onkel* Levi," Eli echoed, following his sister's lead.

"*Gude nacht*, Anna, Eli," Levi replied with a small smile, ruffling Eli's hair as the boy passed by. "Sleep well."

Rachel began to get up from the sofa, but Conrad stepped in.

"I'll put them to bed," he offered, his voice softening as he looked at his children.

Rachel nodded in appreciation. "I will *kumm* and check on you two a little later."

As Conrad led the children out of the room, their small footsteps faded down the hallway, leaving Levi and Rachel alone in the quiet firelit space. They sat in silence though Levi was aware of his sister's eyes on him.

"Levi," she said gently. "You've been very quiet tonight. Are you all right?"

Levi nodded, but the gesture was half-hearted. "I'm fine," he murmured though he knew it wasn't the whole truth.

Rachel, not convinced, leaned forward.

"Levi, you can talk to me, you know. I've known you long enough to tell when something's bothering you."

Levi sighed, his shoulders slumping as he realized there was no point in hiding what he was feeling. Rachel had always been able to see through him. He hesitated and then finally admitted, "It's Hannah."

Rachel's eyes softened with understanding. "I thought it might be. You've been spending a lot of time with her lately."

Levi nodded, his gaze dropping to the floor. "I've fallen in love with her, Rachel. I didn't mean to, but...I couldn't help it. She's kind, strong, and full of life. She's everything I never knew I was looking for."

Rachel smiled gently. "That doesn't sound like something to be sad about, Levi. Have you told her how you feel?"

Levi nodded. "I have, and she feels the same."

"Then what is the problem?" Rachel asked gently.

Levi's expression grew pained as he looked back up at her. "I haven't spent time alone with her since I told her how I feel, but I'm afraid she's already made her choice."

"You mean Daniel?"

Levi nodded.

"Levi," Rachel said softly. "I understand why you feel this way. But life needs to be lived, especially since, as you and I know too well, none of us knows what sorrow or change might lie ahead. *Gott* brought you here to Willowvale for a reason, and He brought Hannah into your life for a reason, too. Don't let this opportunity pass you by."

Levi looked at her, his brow furrowing as he tried to make sense of her words. "So, what are you saying?"

"I'm saying that you need to fight for what you want, Levi. Don't just step back because it's easier or because you're afraid of the consequences. If you love Hannah, if you believe that *Gott* brought you together, then you owe it to both of you to try. It's what our *eldre* would have wanted."

Levi's chest tightened at the mention of their parents, the familiar pang of loss that always accompanied thoughts of them twinging his heart. But with that loss came the memory of their strength and their unwavering belief in living life with purpose and love.

He took a deep breath as Rachel's words resonated deeply within him. "But what if... what if she chooses Daniel? What if I lose her?"

Rachel smiled gently. "That's a risk you have to be willing to take. But if you don't try, you'll always wonder 'what if.' And that, Levi, is something you'll never be able to shake."

Levi fell silent. Rachel's words echoed in his mind, and he knew she was right. He had come to Willowvale searching for a new beginning, and in Hannah, he had found something he didn't even know he was looking for.

Rachel squeezed his hand one more time before letting go. "You've been given a second chance, Levi. Don't let it slip away. *Gott* has a plan for you, and maybe, just maybe, that plan includes Hannah."

Levi sat wordlessly, his mind racing with thoughts of what his sister had said. He knew she was right; he couldn't let fear or doubt keep him from pursuing the life he wanted. The love he felt for Hannah was real, and it was worth fighting for. He couldn't just stand by and let her slip away.

"You're right," he said. "I need to go."

Levi stood up and left the room, grabbing his

coat and scarf as he made his way outside.

He hurried through the snow-covered streets of Willowvale, his breath coming out in quick puffs of steam as he moved. The village was quiet and the lights in most of the houses dimmed as families settled in for the night. But Levi's resolve only grew stronger as he made his way toward the Weavers' place.

When he arrived, it was to a dark and empty house. His heart sank a little at the realization that Hannah must not be home. He paused, uncertainty gnawing at him. But then, almost as if driven by instinct, he turned and started walking again—this time toward the Kings' house.

Levi's thoughts raced as he approached the familiar house. He knew this was where Hannah had likely gone after the sing-along. He wasn't sure what he was going to say, but he knew he had to see her, to speak with her, before it was too late.

When he reached the Kings' front door, he hesitated for only a second before raising his hand and knocking firmly. The sound echoed through the quiet night, and Levi held his breath as he waited.

He heard footsteps on the other side of the door, and it creaked open. Mrs. King appeared in the doorway, her expression one of surprise and confusion. "Mr. Miller," she said, her voice soft but clearly puzzled. "What are you doing here?"

Levi swallowed, trying to steady his nerves. "I'm sorry to disturb you, Mrs. King, but...I need to speak with Hannah. It's important."

Before Mrs. King could respond, Daniel appeared behind her, his face darkening at the sight of Levi standing on his doorstep. "*Maem*, I'll handle this," Daniel said, his voice firm as he gently guided her back into the house.

Mrs. King glanced between the two men, clearly sensing the tension, but she nodded and stepped back, leaving them alone in the entryway. Daniel took a step forward, closing the door behind him to join Levi outside. The two men faced each other, the air between them thick with unspoken words.

"What do you want, Levi?" Daniel asked, his tone cold though his eyes betrayed a hint of wariness.

Levi took a deep breath, trying to remain calm. "I want to speak with Hannah."

Daniel's eyes narrowed, and he shook his

head. "*Nee*, Levi. You can't. Hannah and I are getting married in a few days. It's too late for whatever it is you think you need to say."

Levi's heart clenched at Daniel's words, but he stood his ground. "Daniel, please. I just need to talk to her—"

But Daniel's expression only hardened. He took another step closer, his voice dropping to a more serious timbre. "Levi, I've loved Hannah my entire life. She's everything to me, and I won't lose her. Not now, not after everything we've been through. You came here as a stranger; you don't know her the way I do. You don't understand what she means to me."

A pang of guilt and doubt pierced Levi at Daniel's declaration, but he pushed it aside, focusing on the truth he had come to share. "Daniel, I understand that you love her. But I love her, too. And I can't just walk away—"

Daniel's eyes flashed with anger, but there was also a sadness in their depths. "*Ya,* you can," he challenged. "Walk away and let her be happy; let me make her happy."

The sincerity in Daniel's voice shook Levi, and for a moment, he wavered. Daniel's love for Hannah was irrefutable, and the bond they shared was deep, forged over years of friendship and shared experiences.

"Daniel...I don't want to hurt anyone. I just want what's best for Hannah. But I need to know that she's making her choice freely, that she's following her heart, not just what's expected of her."

Daniel's expression softened slightly, but his resolve remained resolute. "Hannah has made her choice, Levi. She's agreed to marry me, and everything is arranged. We've been through so much together, and I know she loves me. Don't make this harder for her."

"I understand, Daniel. But I need to hear it from her."

"It's late," Daniel replied unwaveringly. "You should go."

"Daniel—"

But Daniel pivoted, opened the door to step inside, and then closed the door with a loud thud, leaving Levi alone on the porch.

Chapter Fifteen

Hannah was seated in the sitting room with her father when she suddenly heard Levi's voice coming from the hallway. Her heart instantly soared, and she felt a surge of hope and anxiety all at once. Without thinking, she started to rise from her seat, her heart racing with the desire to see him, to hear what he had to say.

But before she could fully stand, her father's hand came down gently on her arm, holding her back. Hannah's heart sank as she settled back into her seat, her mind whirling with questions about why Levi could possibly be at the Kings' home.

A few minutes passed, each one feeling interminable. The sound of the door closing reached her ears, and she strained to hear or see any sign of Daniel returning to the room. But he didn't come back.

Hannah couldn't stand the uncertainty a moment longer. She excused herself quietly from the sitting room, her father giving her a stern glance but not stopping her this time. She made her way to the kitchen, her footsteps soft on the wooden floor.

She entered to find Daniel standing there, his back to her. His shoulders were tense, and his hands gripped the kitchen counter's edge as if trying to steady himself. The sight of Daniel like that—so full of tension and pain—cut Hannah to the quick, but she knew she couldn't avoid the truth any longer.

"Daniel," she began softly, her voice barely above a whisper. "What was Levi doing here?"

Daniel didn't turn around at first. His silence was heavy. Finally, he spoke, his voice low and strained. "He came to talk to you."

Hannah took a step closer. "Why didn't you let him? What did he want to say?"

At that, Daniel whirled around to face her, a million emotions flashing across his face— betrayal, anger, hurt, and desperation. "Because we're getting married, Hannah!" he snapped, his voice rising. "I love you! And I won't let him *kumm* in here and ruin everything we've built together."

Hannah flinched at the intensity in his voice, and guilt washed over her at the agony in his expression. She had never wanted to hurt Daniel, but the truth was demanding to be spoken.

"Daniel, I—" she began, her voice trembling.

"You're mine," Daniel asserted, stepping closer to her, his hands clenched at his sides. "We've known each other our whole lives. We've always been meant to be. You can't just throw that away because of some newcomer who doesn't understand what we have."

"Daniel, please listen to me," Hannah pleaded, her voice shaking. "I care about you, I do. You're my best friend, and I've always valued what we have. But…"

"But what?" Daniel demanded, his voice laced with pain. "But you don't love me?"

Tears pricked at the corners of Hannah's eyes.

"I do love you, Daniel," she whispered, her voice thick with emotion. "But not in the way you deserve. Not in the way a *fraa* should love her *mann*."

Daniel's face contorted with pain, and he took a step back as if her words had physically struck him. "So it's Levi, then," he retorted bitterly, his voice trembling with anger and heartbreak. "You're going to choose him over me? After everything we've been through?"

Hannah shook her head, tears sliding down her cheeks. "It's not about choosing between you and Levi. It's about being honest with myself and with you. I've been trying to force myself to feel something that I don't because I didn't want to hurt you or disappoint my father. But I can't do that anymore. It's not fair to either of us."

Daniel's eyes blazed with anger, but beneath it, was a deep, aching sadness. "So, what, Hannah? You're just going to throw everything away? All the years we've spent together, all the plans we've made? You're going to walk away from all of that for a *mann* you barely know?"

Hannah's heart twisted in agony at his words. "I don't want to hurt you, Daniel," she said softly. "But I can't marry you when my heart isn't truly in it. It wouldn't be right or fair for either of us."

Daniel stared at her, his chest rising and

falling with deep, shaky breaths. "History is filled with people who married without being in love, but over time, they came to love one another deeply. If there is even a hint of love between us, we can make it work and have a happy marriage."

"*Ya*, Daniel," Hannah replied sincerely. "That is true. *Gott* blesses the union between a *mann* and *fraa*, especially when they pledge to a life together out of a shared love for Him. But the Bible also admonishes us to be wise and to seek *Gott's* will and direction in the big decisions of our lives. And you forget that history is also full of broken hearts where true love had to be cast aside for the sake of politically advantageous unions, where lifelong unhappy marriages caused heartbreak. Would you really want to spend a lifetime with me, knowing that my heart belongs to someone else before we even start?"

Daniel let out a long, pained sigh. "I've loved you my whole life, Hannah," he said quietly, his voice breaking. "I thought...I thought you felt the same way."

The ensuing silence between them was filled with a shared history and dreams that were crumbling to pieces.

"I'm so sorry, Daniel," Hannah whispered. "I never wanted to hurt you. You mean so much to me. I care for you, and I love you dearly as a friend, but I can't marry you out of obligation. It wouldn't be fair to either of us."

Daniel turned away from her, his shoulders slumping in defeat.

"I just want things to go back to how they were between us," Hannah voiced sadly.

Daniel shook his head. "We can't go back," he said. "Only forward."

Then, without another word, Daniel walked out of the kitchen, leaving Hannah standing there alone.

As she wiped the tears from her eyes, Hannah heard the sound of footsteps behind her. She turned slowly, her breath hitching when she saw her father standing in the doorway.

Bishop Weaver's face was stern, his expression unreadable. He looked at her, his eyes cold, distant. He didn't say anything, just stood there, his presence filling the small kitchen with an oppressive silence.

"It's time to go," he finally said, his tone flat and impassive.

Hannah's heart sank even further at his distant manner. She nodded, unable to find words to respond. She followed him out of the Kings' house, her steps heavy and reluctant.

Father and daughter walked home in silence. The path home felt longer than usual. The silence between them stretched out, swollen with unspoken words. Hannah kept her eyes on the ground, unable to bear the thought of looking at her father and seeing the disappointment she knew was there.

When they finally reached their home, Bishop Weaver opened the door and stepped inside, holding it open for Hannah to follow. She did so, her heart heavy as she crossed the threshold.

Her father closed the door behind them, with the sound of the latch clicking into place echoing in the stillness. He turned to face her, his expression hardening even more.

"Hannah," he began, his voice low and controlled. "You embarrassed me tonight. And you embarrassed the Kings."

The words cut deep like a knife twisting in her chest. Hannah winced, and her eyes filled with tears again. "*Vadder*, I never intended to hurt or embarrass anyone," she explained, her voice trembling.

Bishop Weaver's eyes narrowed, his disappointment clear. "Intentions don't change the outcome, Hannah. Daniel has loved you for years. You know how much this meant to him, how much we all expected this marriage. And yet you chose tonight, of all nights, to humiliate him."

Hannah shook her head as tears trickled down her cheeks. "I wasn't trying to humiliate him or hurt anybody. I just...I couldn't go through with it. It wouldn't have been right."

"Right?" Her father's voice was sharp, laced with anger. "What's right is honoring the commitments we make, Hannah. What's right is respecting the bonds we've built in this *gmay*. Daniel has been nothing but *gut* to you, and this is how you repay him?"

"I care about Daniel, but I don't love him the way a *fraa* should love her *mann*. I couldn't marry him knowing that. It wouldn't have been fair to him. Or to me."

Her father's face remained inexpressive, unmoved by her plea. "Fairness is doing what's best for everyone, not just yourself. You've caused pain and division where there should have been joy. Do you think Daniel deserves this? Do you think our *familye* deserves this?"

Hannah felt as though her heart was being torn in two. But what could she say that she hadn't already said?

Her father shook his head, his expression softening marginally. "Go to bed, Hannah. We'll talk more in the morning."

She turned toward the stairs, her feet feeling like lead as she climbed each step.

When she reached her room, she closed the door behind her and leaned against it; the tears she had been holding back finally gave way. She slid down to the floor, her body shaking with sobs as the enormity of what had happened crashed down on her.

Hannah felt utterly alone. She had done what she believed was right, but in doing so, she hurt the people she cared about most. The pain of that realization was almost unbearable.

Hannah crawled into bed, pulling the covers up to her chin in a subconscious bid to shield herself from her turmoil. But the tears kept coming, a product of the heartbreak and confusion that filled her. As she lay there, the darkness of the room closed in around her, and Hannah cried herself to sleep.

∞ ∞ ∞

The next morning, one could almost cut the tense atmosphere at home with a knife. Hannah could feel it the moment she woke up, the memories of the previous night coming back to her and hanging over her like a dark cloud. Her father's words echoed in her mind as taunting reminders of the disappointment she had caused. She could barely bring herself to face him as she went about her morning routine, the silence between them more oppressive than any argument could have been.

Bishop Weaver was silent, his movements deliberate as he prepared for the day. He didn't look at Hannah or even speak, and his cold demeanor only made Hannah's heart ache all the more. She made one attempt to speak to him, to apologize, to explain, but he simply shook his head and walked away, leaving her standing there, feeling utterly alone.

Unable to bear the stifling atmosphere any

longer, Hannah decided she needed to escape, to clear her mind and find some semblance of peace, if only for a little while. Without a word, she grabbed her shawl and coat and slipped out the door, her footsteps hurried as she made her way out of the house.

The streets of Willowvale were quiet. The village still had the sleepy, peaceful air of a community just waking up, but for Hannah, there was no peace to be found. Her heart was heavy, her thoughts swirling with guilt, regret, and uncertainty.

When she reached the bakery, she removed the keys from her apron pocket and let herself in, grateful for the solitude. The bakery was closed for the day, but Hannah kept herself busy mopping the floor and cleaning the counters. Unexpectedly, the small bell above the door jingled.

"Sorry," she called. "We're not open today."

Hannah looked up from behind the counter, surprised to see Levi. Though she was physically fatigued and emotionally and mentally exhausted, her heart skipped a beat at the sight of him.

"Hannah," Levi said softly as he stepped

inside, closing the door behind him. "I've been looking for you."

Hannah wiped her wet hands on her apron and forced a smile though it didn't reach her eyes. "I just needed to get out of the house," she said quietly.

Levi walked over to her. "What happened?"

Hannah's forced composure crumbled, and she let out a shaky breath as she leaned against the counter. "Daniel and I argued, and...I told him the truth. That I couldn't marry him because I didn't love him the way he deserved to be loved."

Levi's gaze softened, and he stepped closer, his hand gently resting on her arm. "I'm sorry, Hannah. I know that must have been so difficult for you."

Hannah nodded, tears welling up in her eyes. "My *vadder*...he's so disappointed in me, Levi. He said I embarrassed him and the Kings. I never wanted to hurt anyone, but I couldn't keep pretending. I couldn't live a lie."

Without hesitation, he pulled her into his arms. Hannah let herself be held and let the warmth and strength of Levi's embrace offer the comfort she so desperately needed. She buried her face in his chest, the tears she had been holding back spilling over.

"It's going to be all right," Levi murmured, his voice soothing as he held her close. "You did the right thing even if it doesn't feel like it right now."

Hannah clung to him, her voice trembling as she whispered, "How, Levi? How will it be all right when everything feels so horrid?"

Levi pulled back just enough to look into her eyes, his expression filled with determination and a quiet resolve. "*Kumm* with me, Hannah."

Hannah blinked, her brow furrowing in confusion. "Where are we going?"

"To talk to your *daed*," answered Levi.

∞∞∞

Hannah stood in the living room of her home, her heart pummeling her sternum as she watched Levi and Bishop Weaver in a faceoff. Hannah's hands were clasped tightly in front of her, her knuckles white as she waited in nervous anticipation.

Bishop Weaver's expression was formidable,

his arms crossed over his chest as he regarded Levi. "Haven't you caused enough trouble for my *dochder* and our *familye*?"

Levi took a deep breath, his eyes steady as he met Bishop Weaver's gaze. "I know you're upset, Bishop Weaver," Levi began, his voice calm but filled with emotion. "And I understand why. I never intended to cause trouble, and I never wanted to hurt anyone, least of all Hannah. But there's something I need to say, and I hope you'll hear me out."

Bishop Weaver's eyes narrowed slightly, but he didn't interrupt. He simply stood there, his expression guarded as he waited for Levi to continue.

Levi took a step forward, his gaze never leaving Bishop Weaver's. "I love Hannah," he said, his voice steady and sincere. "I know you don't know me well, and I know I'm not who you might have envisioned for your *dochder*—"

"*Nee*," Bishop Weaver agreed.

"My *eldre* married for love," Levi continued. "They taught me to follow my heart, to seek out the kind of love that is true and lasting. They weren't perfect, but they loved each other deeply, and they raised me to believe that love—real love

—is worth fighting for."

Bishop Weaver's expression remained stern, but something else flickered in his eyes, something that made Hannah's heart leap with hope.

"I came to Willowvale for a fresh start, and I never intended to fall in love with Hannah," Levi continued, his voice thick with emotion. "But I did. And now that I have, I can't imagine my life without her. I will love her with everything I have for as long as I live."

Levi's words hung in the air, a quiet plea that was filled with honesty and vulnerability. Hannah could see her father's struggle, being torn between his desire to protect her and the undeniable sincerity in Levi's voice.

A long silence passed, with the tension in the room reaching its peak as Bishop Weaver considered Levi's words. His expression remained indecipherable, and his gaze remained fixed on Levi as if searching for any hint of insincerity.

Eventually, after what felt like an eternity, Bishop Weaver's stiff posture relaxed ever so slightly. He let out a long, measured breath, his gaze softening vaguely as he looked between Levi and his daughter.

"You speak of love with a great deal of conviction," Bishop Weaver said quietly, his voice no longer harsh but contemplative. "And I can see that you mean what you say. But love alone is not enough to build a marriage. It takes trust, respect, and a willingness to work through the hard times."

Levi nodded, his expression earnest. "I understand that, sir. And I'm willing to put in the work. I know that life isn't always easy and that love can be tested in ways we can't predict. But I'm committed to Hannah, to building a life with her that's founded on love, trust, and mutual respect."

Bishop Weaver studied Levi for a moment longer, the silence between them intense with unspoken thoughts. Then, slowly, he turned his gaze to Hannah.

"Hannah. May I have a word, alone?"

She nodded, her throat tightening with anxiety.

They stepped into the study off the main room, and Bishop Weaver closed the door behind them.

"Hannah," her father began, turning to face

her.

"*Vadder*," Hannah interjected. "Before you say anything, will you let me talk?"

Bishop Weaver hesitated, then nodded.

"I understand your concerns," she started, her voice steady despite the turmoil in her heart. "But Levi isn't a stranger to me. He may be new to Willowvale, but he's not new to my heart. I've *kumm* to know him well, and I love him."

Bishop Weaver's eyes narrowed, and his brow furrowed in disapproval. "Love, Hannah? Love isn't always enough. How can you be sure that's what you feel for Levi, anyway, when you've only known him a short while?"

Hannah took a deep breath, feeling the familiar fear of disappointing her father rising within her. But she pushed it down, determined to make him understand. "Since *Maem* died, I've been so scared of disappointing you, of not living up to your expectations, that I've done whatever I can to please you. I was willing to marry Daniel —even though I knew deep down he wasn't right for me. I thought it would make you proud, that it would make you happy."

Her voice wavered slightly, but she pressed on, feeling emboldened as the first step opened the way for the truth to pour out in a rush. "But I can't marry someone just to make you happy. I have to follow my heart, and my heart is with Levi. Can't you see that?"

Bishop Weaver's stern expression faltered, a flicker of uncertainty crossing his face. He opened his mouth to respond, but Hannah continued, her words gaining strength as she spoke.

"I know you mean well, *Vadder*," Hannah said gently, taking a step closer to him. "You've always tried to protect me, to guide me in the right direction. But you need to listen to me now. I'm not a *maedel* anymore. I need to make my own choices, and I need you to trust me. Trust that I know what's best for me and that I'm following *Gott's* plan for my life."

Bishop Weaver sighed deeply and regarded his daughter.

"Hannah, I've always tried to do what's best for you. It's hard for me to let go, to trust that you're making the right decision, especially when it comes to something as important as marriage."

Hannah nodded, sympathetic to the struggle he was facing. "I know," she said. "And I appreciate everything you've done for me. But I need to live my own life, to make my own choices —even if that means making mistakes along the way. I believe that Levi is the one for me. I know it in my heart."

Bishop Weaver studied her, his eyes searching hers as if looking for some sign to reassure him. Finally, he nodded slowly, the lines of his face softening in acceptance.

"I suppose," he said quietly, "that it's time I let you make your own choices. I don't want to lose you, Hannah. I just want to make sure you're happy."

A rush of relief and gratitude washed over Hannah, her eyes filling with tears. "I am happy. And I will be even happier if you can accept Levi and *willkumm* him into our *familye*."

Bishop Weaver hesitated, then gave her a small smile. "If Levi is who you've chosen, then I'll do my best to accept that. I want what's best for you, Hannah. I'll try to trust in your decision."

"*Danki, Vadder*. That means more to me than you know."

As they left the study together, the tension between them eased. They entered the sitting room again, and Levi turned to them.

"Would you like to stay for some lunch, Levi?" Bishop Weaver asked. "If you are planning on marrying my *dochder,* I'd like to get to know you a bit better."

Levi's eyes widened in surprise as he did his best to suppress his grin. "I would like that very much!"

Bishop Weaver nodded as he turned and exited the room. Once he was gone, Hannah turned to Levi.

"You did it," he said, holding her gaze. "You convinced him."

Hannah grinned as she hurried into his arms. "All I did was speak from the heart. And I meant every word. I love you, Levi Miller, and I intend to live the best life with you."

Levi smiled as he leaned down and dropped a gentle kiss on her lips.

"Well, I prayed for a *Grischtdaag* miracle," Hannah said breathlessly with a grin. "And I got one."

Epilogue

Three Years Later

A roaring fire and the gentle hum of laughter and conversation filled the house with warmth. Mary sat in her favorite armchair, a needle and thread in hand, carefully stitching a square of fabric that had once been part of Grace's favorite dress. The fabric was worn, but its pattern was still vibrant—a delicate floral print that brought back memories of her daughter's laughter and her tiny hands reaching out to touch the flowers as she played.

Over three years had passed since that dark winter when she and Isaac almost lost everything. Now, as the snow gently fell outside, blanketing Willowvale in a serene, peaceful white, Mary's heart was full—of love, gratitude, and the joy that came from being surrounded by the people she cherished most.

The quilting circle had become a tradition in the community, a gathering of women who came together not just to sew but to share their lives, their stories, and their memories. This year, they were working on a special project: a memory quilt. Each square represented a loved one—someone who had touched their lives, someone who had been lost, or someone they wanted to honor. The quilt was a way to keep their memories alive, to stitch their stories into something tangible and lasting.

Mary looked around the room at the women who had become like sisters to her. Hannah was there, sitting across from her, her hands deftly stitching a square that bore the initials of her and Levi's first child, a little girl named Grace—after the daughter Mary and Isaac had lost. Hannah's face was serene, her smile soft as she listened to the stories being shared around the room.

Levi and Hannah married in the spring following that crucial Christmas, and their love had blossomed into something truly beautiful. Mary had watched with joy as their family grew, as they welcomed a child into their lives and built a home filled with love and laughter. Levi was now a beloved member of the community, with his carpentry skills and his gentle heart earning him the respect of everyone in Willowvale.

Mary's gaze shifted to Ruth, who was carefully stitching a square that represented her late husband, Timothy. He had passed peacefully a year earlier, and though his absence was deeply felt, Ruth's strength and faith carried her through the grief. The square she was working on was from one of Timothy's old work shirts, the fabric faded and soft from years of wear.

As the women sewed, the atmosphere was filled with the soft murmur of voices, the sharing of stories that brought laughter, and sometimes, tears. It was a time of reflection, of honoring those who had come before, and of celebrating the lives they had touched.

"I remember when Grace was just a *boppli*," Mary said softly, her voice filled with the warmth of fond memories. "She used to love this dress. She'd twirl around in it, and the skirt would flare out like a little bell. She was so full of life, so full of joy."

Hannah looked up from her stitching

and smiled at Mary, her eyes shining with understanding. "She brought so much light into this world, Mary. And through this quilt and her memory, she'll continue to do so."

The women nodded in agreement, their hands moving in synchrony as they stitched their squares. The quilt was more than just fabric and thread; it was a tapestry of their lives, a collection of memories that bound them together as a community.

As the evening wore on, the stories continued to flow—some funny, some poignant, all of them woven into the fabric of the quilt. There was laughter, the kind that bubbled up from deep within and spread warmth through the entire room. There were moments of quiet reflection, when a story touched a chord in someone's heart and the room would fall silent, each woman lost in her own thoughts.

The quilt grew as the night wore on, each square a piece of the past stitched into the present, creating a tapestry of love and remembrance. When the final stitch was made, the women gathered around the quilt, their hands joined in a circle, their hearts full.

"We've all lost someone," Ruth said softly,

her voice filled with the wisdom of years. "But through this quilt, we keep them close. We keep their memories alive. And we honor them by continuing to live, to love, and to share our lives with each other."

Mary felt a deep sense of peace as she looked at the quilt, at the squares that represented so much love, so much history. This quilt would be passed down through generations, each stitch a reminder of the lives they had lived, the people they had loved, and the community that had supported them through it all.

The evening ended with hugs and warm goodbyes, the women wrapping themselves in their shawls and stepping out into the crisp night air.

As the last of the quilting women left for their homes, the house slowly quieted, settling into the comfortable rhythm of family life. Mary stood in the kitchen, busy preparing Christmas Eve dinner.

Hannah remained behind with Mary, her presence in the kitchen a familiar comfort. Little Grace played happily around their feet, her giggles filling the room with a joy that made Mary's heart swell. Hannah and Levi's daughter was a vibrant, curious child, with her mother's soft curls and her father's bright eyes. She was a constant reminder of the continuity of life.

"Careful there, little one," Hannah said with a smile, gently nudging Grace away from the stove, where she was stirring a pot of rich stew. "We don't want you getting hurt."

Grace looked up at her mother with an innocent expression.

"Why don't you help me put these carrots in the bowl?" Mary suggested, handing a small bowl down to Grace.

The little girl took it eagerly, carefully placing the chopped carrots into the bowl, her small hands moving with careful concentration. Hannah watched her daughter with a tender smile, her heart full as she saw the bond forming between Mary and Grace.

As the final touches were put on the meal, the double click of the back door opening and closing signaled Isaac and Levi's arrival. The two men came in from the workshop, their hands and clothes covered with fine sawdust. They had been busier than usual with last-minute crafting of Christmas gifts and decorations.

"Careful, now," Hannah teased with a playful

smile as she turned to face them. "We don't want sawdust in the food. Go on, wash up, the both of you."

Levi grinned, unbothered by the gentle scolding, and scooped up his daughter, who had toddled to greet him with arms wide open. "*Kumm* here, you," he said, lifting her up and planting a kiss on her cheek. Grace giggled and wrapped her arms around his neck, holding him close.

"*Daed!*" she squealed with delight as he spun her around, her curls bouncing with the movement.

Isaac chuckled, watching the scene with a warm smile. "I think she's been waiting for that all day."

"Well, I can't disappoint my favorite little *maedel*, can I?" Levi replied, his eyes filled with love as he looked at Grace. "But your *Maem* is right, we should clean up before supper."

Levi set Grace down, and both men headed to the sink to wash their hands. Their wives shared a secret smile at the sounds of running water and the light-hearted conversation between their husbands. The friendship between the two families was treasured by all of them. When they were done washing up, the men joined Mary and Hannah at the table, where the rich aroma of the meal awaited them.

As they all settled into their seats, Mary glanced around the table, feeling a deep sense of gratitude for the family that surrounded her.

"Did Bishop Weaver not want to join us tonight?" she asked Hannah, noticing the empty chair where her father would normally sit.

Hannah shook her head, a soft smile on her lips. "He wanted to, but Rebecca—Daniel's *fraa*— is expecting their first *boppli*. She asked him to be there to bless the *boppli* when she's born."

Mary nodded in understanding, her heart warmed by the thought of new life being welcomed into the world. "How *wunderbaar*. I'll be sure to keep them in my prayers tonight."

The room fell into a comfortable silence as they all began to eat, the only sounds being the clinking of silverware and the occasional murmur of conversation. The meal was simple and hearty—rich stew, fresh bread, buttered vegetables, and a warm apple pie for dessert. The food filled their stomachs, but it was the company that truly nourished their souls.

As they ate, stories and memories were

shared, each one bringing a smile or a laugh. Mary and Isaac spoke of Christmases past, of the years they had spent together, and of the love and God's faithfulness that had carried them through even the darkest of times. Hannah and Levi shared stories of their early days together, the challenges they had faced, and the joy they had found in building their family.

"Do you remember the first *Grischtdaag* we spent together after we got married?" Isaac asked, his eyes twinkling with the memory.

Mary laughed softly, nodding. "*Ya*, and I remember how you carved that little wooden bird for me. It was the most beautiful thing I had ever seen."

Isaac smiled, reaching out to take her hand. "And you made me that scarf, the one I still wear every winter. It's kept me warm all these years, just like your love."

Levi and Hannah exchanged a glance, their hands entwined on the table. Mary smiled at Isaac. The years had brought challenges, but they also brought so much joy, so much love.

As the meal wound down, the conversation quieted, and they all sat together in the warmth of the room, the flickering light of the fire casting a soft glow across their faces. The love that filled the room was tangible. It gave body to the bonds they had forged and the memories they had created.

Mary looked around the table, her heart full to bursting. This was what she had always dreamed of—a home filled with love, laughter, and the warmth of family. As she met Isaac's eyes, she knew that despite everything they had been through, they had found their way to a place of peace and happiness.

"To *familye*," Mary said softly, raising her glass in a toast. "To the love that binds us together and to the memories we hold dear."

The others raised their glasses. "To *familye*," they all repeated in unison, their voices filled with the love that had brought them to that exact moment.

And as they sat together, sharing that quiet, perfect Christmas Eve, Mary knew that they had all truly found their way home.

Later that night, as Mary and Isaac prepared for bed, the memory quilt folded carefully at the foot of their bed, an overwhelming sense of gratitude bubbled up in her. Life had not been easy, but it had been filled with times of beauty and grace, times that she would carry with her always.

Isaac wrapped his arms around her as they settled into bed, his presence a steady comfort. "Are you happy, Mary?" he asked softly, his voice filled with the quiet concern that had always been part of who he was.

Mary turned to him with eyes aglow with love. "I am, Isaac. More than I ever thought possible. We've been through so much, but we've *kumm* out the other side stronger, closer, more anchored in *Gott*."

He smiled and kissed her forehead, pulling her closer. "I'm glad. I don't know what I'd do without you."

"You'll never have to find out," Mary whispered, her voice full of promise. "We have each other and that's enough."

Thank you, readers!

Thank you for reading this book. It is important to me to share my stories with you and that you enjoy them. May I ask a favor of you? If you enjoyed this book, would you please take a moment to leave a review on Amazon and/or Goodreads? Thank you for your support!

Also, each week, I send my readers updates about my life as well as information about my new releases, freebies, promos, and book recommendations. If you're interested in receiving my weekly newsletter, please go to newsletter.sylviaprice.com, and it will ask you for your email. As a thank-you, you will receive several FREE exclusive short stories that aren't available for purchase!

Blessings,
Sylvia

Books By This Author

An Amish Christmas In Whispering Pines

In the heart of Whispering Pines, where emotions have long been held captive, a tale of rekindled love and hidden family secrets unfolds amidst the magic of Christmas.

For nearly half a century, Ava Fisher has carried the weight of unspoken feelings for her childhood best friend. Now entering their twilight years, can they find the courage to mend old wounds and rekindle a love that has smoldered in the shadows?

Marcus Duncan has vowed to shun romance to protect his heart after seeing how devastated his father was after his mother's passing. As he closes out his father's estate in Scotland, a startling revelation sends him on a quest to Whispering Pines. Could the truth of his mother's Amish roots offer the answers he seeks about her identity?

Sachia Bachman, a grieving orphan, finds solace in Ava's comforting presence as Ava becomes a maternal guide through Sachia's journey to find love. Unexpectedly, a stranger from Scotland requires Sachia's assistance to unite his grandfather with Ava. Can an Englischer unlock the mysteries of love in this tranquil Amish settlement?

This Christmas, join Sylvia Price on an enchanting journey through the snow-covered evergreens of Whispering Pines. Allow her to warm your heart with a story of love's reawakening, newfound affection, and the rekindling of old flames in a place where holiday miracles are known to happen.

The Christmas Cards: An Amish Holiday Romance

Lucy Yoder is a young Amish widow who recently lost the love of her life, Albrecht. As Christmas approaches, she dreads what was once her favorite holiday, knowing that this Christmas was supposed to be the first one she and Albrecht shared together. Then, one December morning, Lucy discovers a Christmas card from an anonymous sender on her doorstep. Lucy receives more cards, all personal, all tender, all comforting. Who in the shadows is thinking of her at Christmas?

Andy Peachey was born with a rare genetic disorder. Coming to grips with his predicament makes him feel a profound connection to Lucy Yoder. Seeking meaning in life, he uses his talents to give Christmas cheer. Will Andy's efforts touch Lucy's heart and allow her to smile again? Or will Lucy, herself, get in his way?

The Christmas Cards is a story of loss and love and the ability to find yourself again in someone else. Instead of waiting for each part to be released, enjoy the entire Christmas Cards series in this exclusive collection!

The Christmas Arrival: An Amish Holiday Romance

Rachel Lapp is a young Amish woman who is the daughter of the community's bishop. She is in the midst of planning the annual Christmas Nativity play when newcomer Noah Miller arrives in town to spend Christmas with his cousins. Encouraged by her father to welcome the new arrival, Rachel asks Noah to be a part of the Nativity.

Despite Rachel's engagement to Samuel King, a local farmer, she finds herself irrevocably drawn to Noah and his carefree spirit. Reserved and slightly shy, Noah is hesitant to get involved in the play, but an unlikely friendship begins to develop between Rachel and Noah, bringing with it unexpected problems, including a seemingly harmless prank with life-threatening consequences that require a Christmas miracle.

Will Rachel honor her commitment to Samuel, or will Noah win her affections?

Join these characters on what is sure to be a heartwarming holiday adventure! Instead of waiting for each part to be released, enjoy the entire Christmas Arrival series at once!

Unexpected Gifts (Amish Hearts In Hopewell Prequel)

Available for FREE on Amazon

In the heart of Hopewell, Indiana, Gabriel Miller tends to his farm, embracing the solitary life he's carved out for himself. But three unexpected visitors, accompanied by a stranger bearing news of his cousin's untimely passing, disrupt his quiet existence. With no one else to turn to, Gabriel takes on the responsibility of raising the orphaned children. Alone and overwhelmed, he grapples with the daunting task of managing his farm while becoming a caregiver to three young souls.

In this tale of unexpected responsibilities and unspoken desires, Anna Burkholder emerges as a beacon of hope. Stepping in to care for the children during the day, Anna, who harbors an unspoken affection for Gabriel, finds herself entangled in a situation that might just offer her a chance at capturing his attention. As Anna and Gabriel navigate the complexities of raising a family, they discover that love has a way of blossoming in the most unforeseen places.

Will their newfound roles bring them closer together, or will the weight of their responsibilities tear them apart?

The Bridge Of Dreams (Lancaster Bridges Prequel)

Available for FREE on Amazon

Discover a world of love, faith, and community in this prequel to an exciting Amish romance series. Follow the Lancaster County Amish as they navigate the challenges of balancing their beliefs with the allure of the wider world.

In a world where expectations and traditions are highly valued, eldest daughter Hannah Fisher's dream of attending college creates a rift within her Amish community. As Hannah struggles to find a balance between her Amish faith and her desire to explore the outside world, tensions rise, and relationships are put to the test. To complicate matters further, Samuel Stoltzfus, Hannah's childhood friend, has his heart set on courting her, making it even harder for her to choose her path.

Meanwhile, younger sister Ruth struggles to reconcile her own dreams with the expectations of the community. Follow Hannah and her sister Ruth through their journey of self-discovery as they navigate the conflict between tradition and change with unexpected twists and turns along the way.

Sarah (The Amish Of Morrissey County Prequel)

Available for FREE on Amazon

Welcome to Morrissey County! This fictional region in Pennsylvania Amish country is home to several generations of strong-willed Amish women who know what they want in life, even if others disagree. Join these women on their search for love and acceptance.

Morrissey County, 1979

Sarah Kauffman has always abided by the

Ordnung, and not only because her father happens to be the town's bishop and would, she feels, disown her if she didn't. But when her mother passes away, she longs to escape the clutches of her father and run away to the Englisch world. When her father wants her to marry someone she doesn't love, Sarah becomes even more desperate to leave.

Jacob Renno, on the other hand, is happy with life on his farm. It keeps him so busy that the older bachelor has no time for love, but on lonely nights, he finds himself longing for a companion.

When Sarah and Jacob meet, there's an instant connection, but things get complicated. Jacob offers to help Sarah with her dilemma, but Bishop Kaufmann insists that she obey his wishes. Will Sarah run off to join the Englisch, or will the handsome farmer give her pause? Will her father disown her or give her his blessing? Find out in this sweet Amish romance as you become immersed in the lives of these Morrissey County residents.

Sarah is the prequel to the Amish of Morrissey County series. Each book is a stand-alone read, but to make the most of the series, you should consider reading them in order.

The Origins Of Cardinal Hill (The Amish Of Cardinal Hill Prequel)

Available for FREE on Amazon

Two girls with a legacy to carry on. A third choosing to forge her own path.

Welcome to Cardinal Hill, Indiana! This quaint fictional town is home to Faith Hochstetler, Leah Bontrager, Iris Mast, their families, and their trades. Faith, Leah, and Iris are united in their shared passion for turning their hobbies within nature into profitable businesses...and finding love! Find out how it all begins in this short, free prequel!

Other books in this series:
The Beekeeper's Calendar: Faith's Story
The Soapmaker's Recipe: Leah's Story
The Herbalist's Remedy: Iris's Story

The Origins of Cardinal Hill is the prequel to the Amish of Cardinal Hill series. Each book is a stand-alone read, but to make the most of the series, you should consider reading them in order.

A Promised Tomorrow (The Yoder Family Saga Prequel)

Available for FREE on Amazon

The Yoder Family Saga follows widow Miriam Yoder and her four unmarried daughters, Megan, Rebecca, Josephine, and Lillian, as they discover God's plans for them and the hope He provides for a happy tomorrow.

The Yoder women struggle to survive after Jeremiah Yoder succumbs to a battle with cancer. The family risks losing their farm and their livelihood. They are desperate to find a way to keep going. Will Miriam and her daughters be able to work together to keep their family afloat? Will God pull through for them and provide for them in their time of need?

A Promised Tomorrow is the prequel to the Yoder Family Saga. Join the Yoder women through their journey of loss and hope for a better future. Each book is a stand-alone read, but to make the most of the series, you should consider reading them in order. Start reading this sweet Amish romance today that will take you on a rollercoaster of emotions as you're welcomed into the life of the Yoder family.

Amish Love Through The Seasons (The Complete Series)

Featuring many of the beloved characters from Sylvia Price's bestseller, The Christmas Arrival, as well as a new cast of characters, Amish Love Through the Seasons centers around a group of teenagers as they find friendship, love, and hope in the midst of trials. ***This special boxed set includes the entire series, plus a bonus companion story, "Hope for Hannah's Love."***

Tragedy strikes a small Amish community outside of Erie, Pennsylvania when Isaiah Fisher, a widower and father of three, is involved in a serious accident. When his family is left scrambling to pick up the pieces, the community unites to help the single father, but the hospital bills keep piling up. How will the family manage?

Mary Lapp, a youth in the community, decides to take up Isaiah's cause. She enlists the help of other teenagers to plant a garden and sell the produce. While tending to the garden, new relationships develop, but old ones are torn apart. With tensions mounting, will the youth get past their disagreements in order to reconcile and produce fruit? Will they each find love? Join them on their adventure through the seasons!

Included in this set are all the popular titles:
Seeds of Spring Love
Sprouts of Summer Love
Fruits of Fall Love
Waiting for Winter Love
"Hope for Hannah's Love" (a bonus companion short story)

Jonah's Redemption (Book 1)

Available for FREE on Amazon

Jonah has lost his community, and he's struggling to get by in the English world. He yearns for his Amish roots, but his past mistakes keep him from returning home.

Mary Lou is recovering from a medical scare. Her journey has impressed upon her how precious life is, so she decides to go on rumspringa to see the world.

While in the city, Mary Lou meets Jonah. Unable to understand his foul attitude, especially towards her, she makes every effort to share her faith with him. As she helps him heal from his past, an attraction develops.

Will Jonah's heart soften towards Mary Lou? What will God do with these two broken people?

Finding Healing (Rainbow Haven Beach Prequel)

Available for FREE on Amazon

Discover the power of second chances in this heartwarming series about love, loss, and a fresh start from bestselling author Sylvia Price.

After the death of her husband, Beth Campbell decides it's time for a fresh start. When she returns to her hometown in Nova Scotia, she discovers a beautiful old abandoned home by the seaside and imagines it as the perfect spot for her to run a bed and breakfast and finally have the chance to write a novel. But when she discovers that the house belongs to Sean Pennington, a man with whom she has a painful history, she begins to doubt her dream.

With the encouragement of her friends and newfound faith, Beth takes a chance on the dilapidated home and hires Sean as a skilled carpenter to help her restore it. As they work together to bring the old house back to life, Beth and Sean's shared history resurfaces, forcing them to confront unresolved feelings and past mistakes. Will they be able to forgive each other and move on, or will their complicated history keep them apart?

Join Beth on her journey of self-discovery and forgiveness. This inspirational series will touch your heart and remind you that it's never too late to start again. It is perfect for fans of uplifting women's fiction and readers who enjoy stories of finding hope and joy in unexpected places.

Songbird Cottage Beginnings (Pleasant Bay Prequel)

Available for FREE on Amazon

Set on Canada's picturesque Cape Breton Island, this book is perfect for those who enjoy new beginnings and countryside landscapes.

Sam MacAuley and his wife Annalize are total opposites. When Sam wants to leave city life in Halifax to get a plot of land on Cape Breton Island, where he grew up, his wife wants nothing to do with his plans and opts to move herself and their three boys back to her home country of South Africa.

As Sam settles into a new life on his own, his friend Lachlan encourages him to get back into the dating scene. Although he meets plenty of women, he longs to find the one with whom he wants to share the rest of his life. Will Sam ever meet "the one"?

Get to know Sam and discover the origins of the Songbird Cottage. This is the prequel to the rest of the Pleasant Bay series.

About the Author

Sylvia Price

Now an Amazon bestselling author, Sylvia Price is an author of Amish and contemporary romance and women's fiction. She especially loves writing uplifting stories about second chances!

Sylvia was inspired to write about the Amish as a result of the enduring legacy of Mennonite missionaries in her life. While living with them for three weeks, they got her a library card and encouraged her to start reading to cope with the loss of television and radio, giving Sylvia a newfound appreciation for books.

Although raised in the cosmopolitan city of

Montréal, Sylvia spent her adolescent and young adult years in Nova Scotia, and the beautiful countryside landscapes and ocean views serve as the backdrop to her contemporary novels.

After meeting and falling in love with an American while living abroad, Sylvia now resides in the US. She spends her days writing, hoping to inspire the next generation to read more stories. When she's not writing, Sylvia stays busy making sure her three young children are alive and well-fed.

Subscribe to Sylvia's newsletter at newsletter.sylviaprice.com to stay in the loop about new releases, freebies, promos, and more. As a thank-you, you will receive several FREE exclusive short stories that aren't available for purchase!

Learn more about Sylvia at amazon.com/author/sylviaprice and goodreads.com/sylviapriceauthor.

Follow Sylvia on Facebook at facebook.com/sylviapriceauthor for updates.

Join Sylvia's Advanced Reader Copies (ARC) team at arcteam.sylviaprice.com to get her books for free before they are released in exchange for honest reviews.

Made in the USA
Columbia, SC
06 November 2024

45809782R00198